MW01147239

Pra
Kim Iverson Headlee

Dawnflight
"Intense."
~*USA Today*

King Arthur's Sister in Washington's Court
"Entertaining."
~*Publishers Weekly*

Liberty
"Epic."
~*Drue's Random Chatter Reviews*

Morning's Journey
"Compelling."
~*CS Fantasy Reviews*

Snow in July
"Astounding."
~*Room With Books*

The Business of Writing

Handwritten inscription:
2/17/17
David,
Best of luck with your writing & publishing!
Kim Iverson Headlee
Stories make us greater.

Kim Iverson Headlee

PENDRAGON
COVE PRESS

Published by
Pendragon Cove Press

The Business of Writing:
Practical Insights for Independent, Hybrid, and Traditionally
Published Authors
Copyright ©2016 by Kim Headlee

ISBN-13: 978-1-5403229-2-0
ISBN-10: 1-54032292-0

10 9 8 7 6 5 4 3 2 1

Cover design Copyright ©2016 by Natasha Brown
Cover photograph: 123RF.com ID 34926816,
"Blank diary, pen, and glasses" ©2016 by pchweat.
Interior art and photographs:
"Der Gemeindeschreiber" ("The Community Writer") by Gemälde von
Albert Anker, 1874, public domain.
"Still-Life with Books" by an unknown Dutch Master, circa 1620,
public domain.
Book of Kells, Folio 19v, The Gospel of Luke, public domain.
Madeline McDowell Breckinridge, circa 1920, public domain.
Motivational image: Depositphotos ID 86051516, ©2015 by zzoplanet.
Young woman reading, Depositphotos ID 69719181, ©2015 by khunaspix.
Man reading newspaper, Depositphotos ID 69202185, ©2015 by GaudiLab.
Photograph of Kim Iverson Headlee ©2006 by Chris Headlee.

The Business of

Writing

Practial Insights for Independent, Hybrid, and
Traditionally Published Authors

CONTENTS

THE END... OR IS IT? 201

PREFACE

IT'S NIGH IMPOSSIBLE for an author-blogger to introduce a unique theme about which to post. It seems
that everyone in the ever-expanding blogosphere pub-
lishes book spotlights of his or her own or others' works,
information about book signings and other events, personal snippets, and tips about the craft of writing.

All of those topics are fine, well, and good; in fact, I blog
along those lines frequently too. To create a signature
theme for my blog, however, I wanted something writing
related and informational but different. So I conducted a
bit of online research:

"Writers should write about the craft of writing," they
said.

"Don't blog about business-related topics," they said.
"No writer will ever read those types of posts," they said.

"Why not?" I said.

Today, more than one year, forty unique topics, seven guest-blogger posts, and two popular in-person workshops later, my "Business of Writing" posts each Wednesday on *The Maze of Twisty Passages* (http://kim-iversonheadlee.blogspot.com) have accounted for more than one hundred thousand page views at an average of nearly two thousand views per post.

That's not too bad, considering the fact that prior to 2013, when I overhauled and rereleased the first novel in my New York–published backlist, *Dawnflight*, my blog wasn't even a gleam in my eye. I decided to take that particular plunge four months after the novel's relaunch.

So either I've been lucky or "they" were wrong.

Now you get to reap the benefits of my publishing journey, even if you already have begun releasing your own titles or have had work published by a small or large press. I've worked with Simon & Schuster, Harlequin, and Dragon Moon Press (a small, independent Canadian publisher) in addition to striking out into the woolly world of independent publishing. I cover topics that fall under the headings of "Organizing," "Packaging," "Presenting," and "Marketing," so I'm certain that you'll find something to learn from the breadth of my experience. I welcome you to join me on the journey to producing better and more marketable books.

1. ORGANIZING

TRADITIONAL ADVICE FOR any business venture dictates "Plan your work and work your plan." The first aspect of that planning entails getting organized. For a writer, business organization can mean everything from incorporation to selecting accounting software. I discuss these topics and more in this chapter.

1A. Lawyers and Incorporating and Accountants, Oh My!

BACK IN 1994 I was working for a small computer consulting company, and I was shopped out to consult on a project for a Very Big Client. After a year on the job, which was my minimum commitment to the consulting group, the client and I realized that it would be a win-win for us to cut out the middleman. I would get a much higher hourly rate but still not charge as much as the middleman was charging to hire me out to the client.

However, the client required that they be invoiced by a corporation, not an individual, so I found a corporate lawyer (there was no LegalZoom (https://www. legalzoom.com/) in those days) who practiced in the county where I was living at the time, and I sat down with him in person to discuss the various small-business corporate options. He is now an owning partner at his firm, and he relocated to the state capital years ago, but he has remained my corporate lawyer to this day. Even though I could save a few hundred dollars a year if I did my own annual corporate filings, it has been worth it to keep him on tap for questions and for handling other, noncorporate, issues.

For precise definitions of sole proprietorship, S corporation, limited liability corporation, and any other small-business options that I may have missed off the top of my head, I suggest that you google the terms. I am not a lawyer and do not wish to mislead anyone.

Per my lawyer's recommendation, I established System Support Services Inc. (S3I) as an S corporation because I wanted my husband to be an equal co-owner for survivorship purposes. If I predecease him, the corporation may continue to exist rather than being taken over by my estate.

The tax implications are that the net value of all corporate income and expenses are passed through to the owners' individual 1040 form(s) each year. The S corporation itself does not pay tax.

In the early days I had hired a freelance certified public accountant to keep my corporate books and submit my business tax filings (not having to pay tax does not excuse the corporation from having to file), but after a few years he shut down his freelance business to become a corporate CPA. By that time, aided by an accounting class I'd taken several years earlier, I had become familiar enough with the process that I felt comfortable buying QuickBooks (https://quickbooks.intuit.com/) to manage my corporate records, and TurboTax Business (https://turbotax.intuit.com/small-business-taxes/; not to be confused with TurboTax Home & Business, though that product might suffice for an unincorporated freelance writer) to compile my annual S corporation tax returns.

The day in 1995 when I met with my lawyer to decide which type of corporation S3I would become, I had not yet sold any manuscripts but had a hunch I was getting close to landing a contract, so I asked whether I would be able to funnel nonconsulting income and expenses through the corporation too. The answer was an emphatic *yes*.

For a writer, setting up a corporation is optional, but for me the main attraction is that it avoids the "hobby" implication during years when sales are, shall we say, less than stellar but expenses remain astronomical. If the Internal Revenue Service deems that your freelance writing is a hobby, then you may deduct only the amount of expenses that equal your writing income for the tax year. A corporation may deduct expenses in excess of income to show a negative profit, though I try to show at least a modest gain every few years to stay out from under IRS scrutiny.

Another attraction as an independent publisher is that Kindle Direct Publishing, Nook Press, Kobo, CreateSpace, IngramSpark, and all the other places where I publish my books keep my corporate tax ID (formally known as the Federal Employer Identification Number) on file, not my social security number. That makes me far less twitchy about the risk of data breaches. And it causes those companies to generate 1099-MISC tax documents made out in the corporation's name, which further supports the business's viability in the eyes of the IRS.

You do not have to be incorporated in order to set up your own press imprint, however. That's covered in this book under the "Packaging" chapter... and the process is a lot easier than you might think.

1B. Writing Expenses, or "Staying Friendly with Your Ex"

DISCLAIMER: As MENTIONED before, I am not a lawyer. I am not a tax specialist or professional accountant either. I am, however, an author with more than a decade and a half of experience running my writing business. In this subsection I share ideas about the types of expenses related to writing and how to manage them. For specific questions, please consult your corporate lawyer, tax specialist, or accountant!

Yes, writing is a business, with expenses as well as income. And it's never too late for you to start organizing those records for Mr. Tax Man if you haven't already begun to do so.

Since I incorporated my computer-consulting practice more than two decades ago and my corporate lawyer gave me the green light to include my writing business, I have kept a series of spreadsheets, one per year, each with separate tabs (worksheets) delineating the major expense categories wherein I record each item. With this information I can then classify the appropriate amounts in QuickBooks whenever I write a check against my corporate bank account to pay myself back for out-of-pocket expenses. It all gets delineated by category in my balance sheet, which comes in very handy for filing my corporate tax return each March.

The major expense categories I track related to writing include:

- **ADVERTISING:** paid mailing lists, print ads, web promotions (blog tours, tweet packages, website design and maintenance, and so forth), booth fees at book fairs and conventions, and contest entry fees (because I'm advertising my book to the judges)
- **BANK Charges:** fees deducted from royalty payments from publishers who pay me via PayPal, currency conversion fees for foreign purchases of writing-related materials such as research books, ATM fees when the cash withdrawal is used for purchasing writing-related goods or services, and bank account servicing fees
- **GIFTS and Charity:** the fair market value of books or other writing-related items donated as door prizes, given to museums, and so forth
- **DUES and Subscriptions:** amounts paid to writers' organizations such as the Authors Guild (https://www.authorsguild.org/) and Romance Writers of America (https://www.rwa.org/), writing-related print and online subscriptions such as *Writer's Digest* (http://www.writersdigest.com/) and *Publisher's Lunch* (http://lunch.publishersmarketplace.com/)
- **INVENTORY:** the cost (including shipping and taxes) of purchasing my books for resale, delineated by book title, edition type (print, audiobook, e-book), and if a print edition, whether it was purchased new or used—I only pay myself back for print edition purchases; the other editions are usually onetime buys to have the e-book or audiobook available on my Android device as "show and tell" at personal appearances
- **MEALS:** the cost of business meals—since this is a

category that's often flagged for audit, I usually don't bother recording those expenses, but I keep the tab in my spreadsheet from year to year just in case I need to record an entry

- **OFFICE Supplies:** self-explanatory, but I do include software purchases in this category, such as my annual purchase of TurboTax for Business, QuickBooks upgrades, and computer supplies such as physical media for archival purposes
- **OUTSIDE Services:** occasional payments made to service personnel such as translators, artists, book cover and layout designers, editors, book trailer designers, web hosting providers, computer repair technicians, and printers of promotional materials
- **POSTAGE:** again, self-explanatory, but I also include the annual fee to maintain a box at my local post office, since that is the address of record for most of my corporate mailings and for fans of my books
- **PROFESSIONAL Services:** annual payments made to professional service personnel such as my corporate lawyer. Back when I first started my company and employed a freelance accountant, I recorded his fees here too. Personal assistants and public relations specialists' fees also fall under this category. Note: You could record all services under one category rather than splitting them out as I have done for decades. In accounting the number one rule is consistency, so I won't be changing my setup, but I encourage you to establish whatever system works best for your business.
- **RESEARCH:** books and other materials purchased in the course of researching my novels—this is not a traditional tax category but one I established because

I wanted to track those purchases separately from purchases logged as office supplies

- **RETURNS:** logged whenever a customer returns an e-book or print book for a refund. This isn't a problem with my books —I see perhaps two e-book returns in a thousand—so I don't track them, but it is a common business expense.
- **TELEPHONE:** for more than twenty years I've been recording half the monthly cost of my landline expense. This was the common wisdom for delineating business versus personal use when I started the practice, and for me it still makes sense because my Internet service is bundled with my landline, and probably 90 percent of my online activity is directly related to writing and promotion. I don't bother to expense my cell phone usage because probably one-third or less is writing related.
- **TRAVEL:** convention registration fees (subcategorized as "Education" for such publishing-industry-only conventions as RWA National), hotel room costs (including housekeeping tips but excluding meals and other incidental charges such as movie rentals), and transportation (air and rail tickets, tolls, parking fees, and automobile mileage)

A side note on the mileage method for automobile deductions: I use mapping software to determine the one-way distance, create separate lines in my spreadsheet for the "to" and "from" legs, and multiply it by the IRS standard business mileage deduction for the given tax year. The "IRS Standard Mileage Rates at a Glance" page (http://www.irs.gov/Credits-&-Deductions/Individuals/Standard-Mileage-Rates-

Glance) gives you the current rate as compared with the previous tax year. To obtain the value for any other tax year, visit http://www.irs.gov/ and search "standard mileage deduction" plus the year you want to look up.

Every item in my spreadsheet is documented with either a paper or electronic receipt.

You might have noticed that I didn't mention expenses related to the "home business" deduction. The reason that I don't bother trying to claim it—even though I am entitled to do so under current tax laws—is because I have no desire to reduce the tax basis of my residence. It's ideal if you rent a house. If you're a homeowner, however, the home business deduction amounts to a "get you now or get you later" tax tradeoff, and I have chosen the "get you now" option so that I don't complicate matters for myself or my heirs when it comes time to sell my home.

Once I have paid myself back for an out-of-pocket expense, I record the date paid in the appropriate place in my expenses spreadsheet, which automatically updates the "amount remaining" fields on the category's worksheet and on the summary worksheet. That way I can see at a glance how much is yet to be repaid in which category for the given year.

This is of course just one way of organizing your expense records. If you use another system that works for you, I would love to hear about it over a tall glass of something cold and frothy sometime.

1C. Corporate Taxes for Authors, or "Shake Your Tax Thing"

IN THIS SECTION and the next, be prepared to see the dreaded *t*-word:

TAXES.

The rigors of paying state and local sales taxes are as varied as the stars, and I recommend that you consult with your regional tax collection office to learn about the amounts and procedures that apply to your sales tax situation. The best advice about Social Security and indeed all other types of taxes for creative freelancers is dispensed by nationally recognized tax expert and attorney Julian Block. If you receive *Romance Writers Report*, the monthly publication of the Romance Writers of America, you may have seen his encapsulation of tax-law changes in the November 2016 issue. Either way, I commend his book *Julian Block's Easy Tax Guide For Writers, Photographers, And Other Freelancers* to your attention (see appendix for ordering information).

In the following pages I discuss filing federal income taxes for corporations and individuals.

If you haven't incorporated, then each April 15 you need to report your writing-related income (all those bazillion 1099-MISC forms generated by KDP and other book e-tailers) and expenses on your individual IRS form 1040. However, first you must ask yourself whether your writing is a hobby or a business.

I must warn you there's no room for fudging the

answer, and an incorrect assessment can be shockingly expensive.

Kelly Keller, president of Circle Legal law firm, offers some excellent advice in this article (http://sheownsit.com/do-you-have-a-hobby-or-business/) published on the *She Owns It* blog. I encourage you to read the entire article, but if you're in a hurry, the biggest takeaway is the application of the "3-of-5 rule"—to whit, you'll be far less likely to raise flags at the IRS if you have earned income from your writing activities in three out of every five years.

I checked out the Circle Legal website (http://www.circlelegal.com/), and their home page gets my thumbs-up for starting out with "We've heard the jokes. How many attorneys does it take to screw in a light bulb... We get it." They advertise a presence in all fifty states as well as worldwide, so if you have any specific questions about tax preparation for authors, or other legal issues, please open a dialogue with Ms. Keller or another attorney of your choice. I have no relationship with either Ms. Keller or her firm; I'm just offering a solution to what can be a trying process of finding the right attorney for your situation.

Although I established System Support Services Inc. for the purpose of invoicing my computer-consulting business clients, I found that shunting my publishing income and expenses through my S corporation was the easiest way to convince the IRS that I was serious about making a profit as a writer.

And although that gives me twice as many reasons to dread having to "shake my tax thing" each year—business taxes must be filed for US income by March 15—I have never looked back.

1D. Individual Taxes for Authors, or "I Like Big Refunds and I Cannot Lie"

INDIVIDUAL INCOME TAX reporting is one of those disgusting but necessary chores, like spring cleaning, that must be done every year... unless you happen to be like my late father-in-law, who left three years worth of income taxes for his executor—and primarily me, the executor's assistant—to file.

Whether or not you have chosen to incorporate your writing business, you are still on the hook to file individual income taxes if you don't meet the IRS requirements that exempt you from filing.

If you skipped the section wherein I discuss writing-related expenses, now would be a good time to bring yourself up to speed on that topic.

On the income side of the paperwork pile exist the 1099-MISC paper or electronic royalty statements from every company who paid you for the books you sold during the previous tax year. These all get reported to the IRS, so if you mislaid or didn't happen to receive one for a particular income source, but you recorded the deposit in your checkbook or ledger, then you need to factor it into your total royalty income.

Note: If you have been paid in US dollars by an e-tailer such as Amazon, Nook Press, Kobo, or Draft2Digital for book sales made in foreign countries, then you do not have to report it as foreign income.

If you have incorporated your writing business and filed corporate taxes, then the data reported on the resulting K-1 statement will flow into your IRS 1040 form in the appropriate areas. You'll have to ask your tax specialist or accountant which specific areas those are. I've been using TurboTax for more than twenty years, and I pay good money for the software to remember those details and stay abreast of the changes for me.

Whether or not you're a US citizen, it's never too late to establish a system of business income/expense organization and tax reporting that works for you. The good news is that once you've invested the thought, time, and effort to set it up, maintaining it on a regular basis is much easier.

1E. The Publication Plan, or "Plans? We Don't Need No Stinkin' Plans!"

I COULDN'T RESIST riffing on the classic line from one of my favorite comedies of all time, *Blazing Saddles*. This was pretty much how I viewed independent publishing when I dived into the waters in 2013, and I don't recommend that approach to anyone.

There were many reasons why I didn't lay out a publication plan, not the least of which being that my father-in-law had just died, my husband the high school math teacher was up to his eyeballs in teaching (not to mention grief) so the lion's share of the estate's administration fell to me, and I latched on to self-publication as a means of retaining my sanity through that complex and exhausting process.

The fact is that a publication plan can help you boost sales and maximize the return on your investment. And your plan doesn't need to be expressed in formal terms if your memory is good, or if you want to bookmark this section.

The major aspects of the publication plan are prepublication, launch, and promotion, and each phase entails a slew of decisions, most of which need to be balanced against your budget, schedule, temperament, and writing career goals.

1E1. Prepublication Decisions to Consider

- THE first aspect involves determining how many publication details—such as e-book creation, conversion, cover design, print edition layout, and audiobook recording—you plan to handle yourself. I share my thoughts about most of these details in the "Packaging" chapter.

- THE next most important considerations are whether to incorporate (discussed earlier in this chapter) and/or establish your own imprint (described in the "Packaging" chapter). Making these decisions ahead of time will reduce your headaches later and will allow you and your books to appear more professional to the reading public.

- WHICH edition formats will you be releasing for your book? The least expensive in terms of prepublication costs is the e-book, followed by audiobook, paperback, and hardcover. There is the matter of foreign-language translations, comics, and graphic novels if your genre lends itself to these types of editions, and then there are some of the more esoteric decisions such as large print editions. Refer to the "Packaging" chapter for more details about the major edition types.

- IF you're releasing your book as an e-book, are you going to stick with Amazon exclusively, or will you be releasing to additional platforms such as Nook, Kobo, Google Play, and Apple's iBooks Store? Since Amazon accounts for at least 75 percent of paid and free downloads for most authors, there's a certain logic to launching a new title in Kindle Unlimited to take advantage of free and "countdown" promotions.

However, given recent developments with regard to their crackdowns on Kindle scam artists, I advise granting Amazon exclusive distribution of your books for no more than six months to minimize the risk of Amazon shutting down your account with no warning, recourse, or chance of reinstatement because you've been unwittingly victimized by a "click farm" (see section 4.0 for more information about this type of automated thievery software).

- ARE you going to pay for professional editing services or not? If you do plan to follow the wise path of hiring professional editorial services, keep in mind that you may need to schedule the delivery of your manuscript to the editor at least three months in advance of your target release date. Refer to the "Packaging" chapter for more thoughts about editing.

- WHAT release date are you shooting for? Publisher sites such as KDP (https://kdp.amazon.com/), Kobo (https://writinglife.kobobooks.com/), Smashwords (https://www.smashwords.com/), and Draft2Digital (https://www.draft2digital.com/) allow the establishment of future publication dates so that your book can collect preorders. At the time of this writing, Nook Press (https://www.nookpress.com/) does not. You can circumvent Nook Press's limitation, however, by distributing your title to Nook using Smashwords, Draft2Digital, or another third-party distributor.

- How do you plan to build buzz about your book? Online using Facebook, Twitter, Pinterest, or other social media platform? By scheduling a "cover reveal" or "preorder party" blog tour or Facebook event? As many of those options as your time, your budget, your family, and your heart can tolerate?

- IF you have a smartphone, create an account at Square (https://squareup.com/) so that you can process credit cards for book sales at your personal appearances. This needs to be done at least a month in advance of your first in-person sales event to give them time to mail you the device (if you can't find one on the shelves of your local Best Buy or Apple store) and for you to tinker with setting your price points, coding sales tax for your state, linking your Square account to your accounting software, and so forth.
- ESTABLISHING a separate bank account for processing online transactions such as Square, KDP, and other deposits, as well as for paying writing-related expenses is not mandatory, but I have taken this step as a precaution against online theft, and I do recommend it even if you don't incorporate your writing business.

1E2. The Book Launch

- WHERE do you plan to announce your release? On Facebook, Twitter, Pinterest, your blog, or other preferred social media platforms? Schedule online events at least a month in advance.
- I strongly recommend scheduling a "release blitz" blog tour at least two months in advance of your planned release date to maximize the number of reviews your book will receive at the time of launch. Reviews cannot be posted for books in the preorder phase, so having reviews lined up and ready to post on launch day becomes crucial, since many book-promotion sites have minimum requirements for the number of reviews a book has (and often a minimum

star rating) before they will feature it.

- Do you plan to announce the launch at a personal appearance such as a fan convention? If so, then you need to have physical advertising material—book-marks, book cards, or swag—prepared to hand out as well as any vinyl banners or other advertising tools you plan to display.

PROMOTION, SOME of which I touched on above, is an entire activity unto itself. Refer to the "Marketing" chapter for in-depth advice regarding the myriad aspects of book promotion.

1F. Copyrighting Your Book, or "It's Mine! Mine, Mine, Mine, Mine, Mine!"

Now that Daffy Duck has safely squirreled away his jewel for another day, it's quiet enough to speak to you about an administrative chore that may or may not be part of your publication plan: the book's copyright.

1F1. The Basics

You do not have to register your book's copyright. From the moment it exists in tangible or digital form, your work is automatically protected under US copyright law. Simply affix a notice in the frontmatter using this format:

Copyright ©20xx by Your Name

If you don't have access to the © symbol, it's acceptable to substitute the text equivalent: (c)

That's all there is to it.

Under Title 17 of the US Code (Copyright Law of the United States), copyright of an author's work "endures for a term consisting of the life of the author and 70 years after the author's death." There are exceptions for works of various types that were created before certain dates, but the lifetime plus seventy years duration is the general rule.

The full contents of Title 17 may be viewed using this web page: http://www.copyright.gov/title17/. For your convenience, it's organized by chapter, and you have the opportunity to download Title 17 in its entirety as a PDF file. Each chapter may be viewed either as HTML or as a PDF file.

1F2. The Next Level

ALTHOUGH ALL created works enjoy automatic copyright protection, registering the copyright is a means of formally establishing the date of creation, which then becomes crucial in winning a plagiarism lawsuit. All traditional publishers and most small presses exercise this option for every book they publish.

If your book is ready to be released into retail channels, or it already has been, and you wish to secure the next level of protection for your book, registering the copyright may be accomplished as follows:

1. VISIT the Electronic Copyright Office (http://www.copyright.gov/eco/), affiliated with the Library of Congress, and establish an account.
2. ON the left-hand menu, under the category "Copyright Registration," in most cases you will select "Register a New Claim." A *claim* in this context means that you as author or publisher are claiming that the copyright of the work should be registered to you (or the author you represent, if you're a publisher). It has nothing to do with claiming copyright infringement.
3. FOLLOW the prompts to describe the work being registered. The help files are quite extensive and will open in a new tab for your continued reference. In addition, the eCO home page contains links to tutorials and other tools.

4. PAY the appropriate processing fee (as of this writing, $35.00 for a single claimant or $55.00 for multiple claimants per title for online registration, regardless of whether you are required to mail physical copies of the book or are entitled to upload the digital version). Payment is accomplished via pay.gov, the secure payment site operated by the US Treasury Department, and you may choose to pay by electronic funds transfer from your bank account or by credit card. You must scroll down the page until you get to the credit card payment option. For more information, refer to *Circular 4, Copyright Office Fees* (http://www.copyright.gov/fls/sl04.pdf).

5. SUBMIT the required number of copies of your work. If it is only published electronically, you may upload a qualifying digital file. However, if your book exists in print as well as e-book editions and it is already published, then you must mail two copies of the "best edition" within thirty days to the Library of Congress at the address they provide during that phase of the registration process.

You may mail a paper application for copyright registration of your book (*Form TX*; http://www.copyright.gov/forms/formtx.pdf) in lieu of submitting an electronic application. This process costs at least $85.00 per title; and you must submit the application, registration fee, and requisite physical copies together in the same package. *Form TX* contains concise instructions, however, making it a good basic reference if you don't possess the time or patience to wade through eCO's online tutorials and FAQs.

Once your books have been received and processed,

the Copyright Office will mail you a certificate of registration. Eventually. The current advertised processing time for electronic copyright applications is as much as eight months, and users are advised to allow up to fourteen months for processing paper copyright applications.

The eCO website is a bit cumbersome, but it's possible to create templates if you expect to be registering several titles containing much of the same data, such as author name and contact information.

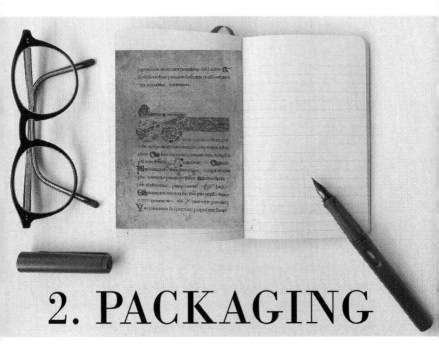

2. PACKAGING

BOOK PACKAGING MAY include obtaining ISBNs and the establishment of a publishing imprint, decisions about editing and formatting the various editions, the use of materials in your book that have been copyrighted by someone else, the book's description, and its cover.

2A. ISBNs and Imprints Demystified

2A1. The ISBN

THIS IS the acronym for International Standard Book Number, a unique commercial book identifier that is now most commonly thirteen digits. For books, the first three digits of the ISBN are 978. Buy ISBNs in bulk from Bowker (https://www.myidentifiers.com), the central authority for assigning ISBNs in the US, because each edition (e-book, paperback, hardcover, graphic novel, etc.) requires a separate ISBN. You will chew through them fast if you are creating several editions of the same title. If you live outside the US, check with your national government's ISBN agency for local application procedures and associated fees, if any. As of this writing, Canada and Mexico assign ISBNs at no charge to the applicant.

There exist differing opinions regarding whether to assign a separate ISBN to the same manuscript file you publish on different e-book platforms (e.g., KDP, Nook, iBooks, Kobo, Google Play, Smashwords, and Draft2Digital). Smashwords insists that the best practice is to assign a unique, unused ISBN to any manuscript you publish with any given e-tailer (source: https://www.smashwords.com/dashboard/ISBNManager). While that will indeed cover your bases, it could become extremely expensive. I maintain that using the same ISBN for different e-tailer versions of the same e-book is valid because the customer's experience is identical in terms of the book's content across all e-reader platforms. If you elect to err on the side of ISBN caution, do avail yourself of the free ISBN that Smashwords and other e-tailers offer.

If your plan is to distribute only on Amazon, then you do not need to buy an ISBN for your e-book because Amazon's internal 10-digit ASIN suffices as a substitute in their system, and you can obtain a free ISBN from Amazon if you release the print edition via CreateSpace. Amazon's newest print-on-demand service, KDP Print—currently in beta as of this writing—also offers a free ISBN.

In 2015 there was a change to European value-added tax law—not yet adopted by all European Union members—that allows for the VAT to not be deducted from your royalty if your e-book has an ISBN. Therefore, you may wish to consider assigning an ISBN to your e-book, especially if you anticipate a great many sales in the EU. The VAT deducted for one $0.99 e-book currently amounts to about three pennies.

If you can afford to pay Bowker $600.00, give or take, for a clutch of one hundred ISBNs, that's the most economical route short of buying one thousand or more. Bowker's next-lowest bulk tier is ten ISBNs for $295.00 as of this writing. Bowker does offer discounts from time to time.

2A2. Imprints

AN *IMPRINT* is publisher-speak for a label to define a body of work. Traditional publishers, such as Simon & Schuster, have established imprints for decades. For example, *Dawnflight* was published in 1999 by Sonnet

Books, a Simon & Schuster imprint for mainstream romance novels.

The process for establishing an imprint is as easy as one-two-three:

1. DECIDE on a catchy name for your imprint (e.g., Pendragon Cove Press).
2. DO your homework to make sure someone else hasn't already decided that it's a catchy name (e.g., Pendragon Cove Press is my imprint). Homework includes any or all of the following steps, depending on how big of a network reach you wish for your imprint to claim:
   A. Search for the name on a book e-tailer site such as Amazon. This step is a must. For example, the Amazon search results for "Pendragon Cove Press" may be viewed using this link: http://www.amazon.com/s/ref=nb_sb_noss?url=-search-alias%3Daps&field-keywords=Pendragon+Cove+Press.
   B. Perform a WHOIS (https://www.whois.net/) lookup if you're interested in purchasing one or more related domains. For now, http://pendragoncovepress.com points to my blog. That's all you need to do if you don't have time to set up a separate web presence for your imprint.
   C. Search Gmail, Ymail, and so forth if you want to claim the imprint's name for one or more email accounts.
   D. Search for your desired imprint's name on Twitter, Facebook, and other social media platforms if you wish to extend the network reach of your imprint in that manner.

3. SEND an email to Bowker requesting that the name be added to their imprints database. They include a "mailto:" hyperlink for this purpose on the page for defining prices when you're setting up your book's ISBN information. I cannot speak to their response time these days, but a Bowker representative got my Pendragon Cove Press imprint established in their database within twenty-four hours in 2014.

Once your imprint is established, then it will display as an option in your book's "publisher" field on the title setup page. This is important, because assigning your given name as publisher blares the "I Am an Indie Author-Publisher" label to God and everybody, which carries the unwanted potential of losing sales.

If you don't create an imprint but have elected to incorporate (refer to the "Organizing" chapter) and have linked your corporate tax ID to your vendor accounts, then your corporation's name will be recorded as the publisher by default. That choice doesn't blare quite so loudly, but establishing one or more imprints for your books will make you appear that much more professional and perhaps give you a leg up on your competition.

Once you have submitted a new-imprint request, please use a little common sense and courtesy in your follow-up correspondence if you believe it's taking too long. I presume that the Bowker employees don't perform those sorts of tasks on weekends and US holidays.

2B. Professional Editing, or "I Do Not Think That Word Means What You Think It Means"

It's not inconceivable for you to slap together a collection of words, dash off a do-it-yourself cover, upload it all to Amazon, and call yourself an author. You might even make some money doing so, and congratulations if that happens to be the case.

Being a professional author, however, entails ever so much more than the technical definition of "earning money for one's efforts" implies.

One of the biggest complaints I hear—and see—with books written by independent authors is the sheer volume of grammar, punctuation, and spelling mistakes. In fact I would go as far as to suggest that poor editing is a leading contributor toward the subpar reputation of independently published books as a whole.

Mistakes will catapult a reader out of a story, perhaps never to return. If you believe your readers won't notice or care about poor editing, then I respectfully suggest that you are underestimating—and alienating—a large sector of your audience.

That's not a risk that I'm willing to take with my own books, and I hope you agree.

To be fair, books churned out by the largest traditional publishers such as Simon & Schuster and Harlequin often contain glaring errors too. The first edition of my novel *Liberty*, published by Harlequin imprint HQN Books in

2006, contained sections of missing and repeated pages in three different combinations, which proved to be quite the nightmare when I was trying assemble good copies to send to reviewers and to sell during personal appearances. That was a printing issue rather than an editing issue, of course, but it's a graphic illustration of my point that mistakes occur at even the highest levels of the publishing business.

The bottom line is that authors who are contracted by large publishing houses already enjoy a level of respectability that's built into the system. The rest of us must do our level best to achieve respectability based on our own merits, and the first step toward that goal is to hire a high-quality professional editor, and perhaps even two if your budget can tolerate it: one for content editing and one for copyediting.

My primary editor is Deb Taber (http://www.deb-taber.com/editing-services), and I cannot say enough good things about her work. She is the consummate professional, she knows the English language inside and out, including the application of actual and author-invented dialects, and she offers encouragement along with fantastic suggestions for improvement. I get nothing for mentioning her here other than the satisfaction of knowing that you will receive the highest quality feedback if you choose to hire her to edit your manuscript... even if a potential drawback is having to compete with more authors for her time.

Someone else whom I commend to your attention is Robin Allen of Griffin Editorial Services (http://griffineditorial.com/). I have known Robin for more than fifteen years, and all the copyediting work she has ever done for me has been top-notch. Again, I get nothing for the mention other than knowing that you will be as delighted with her editing services as I have been.

You say you cannot afford to hire a good editor?

I say you cannot afford not to.

Budget for it, or set up a crowdfunding campaign if you must, but please do not be tempted by those who claim that you can successfully edit your own work. The fact is that the human brain is wired to see what it expects to see, thereby making it impossible to remain objective during the editorial process. Take it from someone who witnessed this phenomenon firsthand for decades while working as a software engineer.

I implore you to help halt the downward spiral in perception of the quality of independent authors' books by hiring professional help to make your manuscript be the absolute best product that it can be.

2C. All's Fair in Love and War But Not When Using Photographs and Other Copyrighted Materials in Your Book

MUSIC IS—QUITE LITERALLY—IN my blood. My great-great-granduncle was Nikolai Rimsky-Korsakov, Russian composer of what is arguably the most famous ninety seconds in all of music history: "The Flight of the Bumblebee."

Much as the four-year-old Nikolai was already becoming accomplished at playing the drums, I began singing in choirs at about the same age. Later in life I would gravitate toward groups that performed classical oratorios, and I helped to found an oratorio society in North Carolina in the early 1990s.

Thus it was only natural that I also developed a talent for composing original lyrics to popular tunes to serve as outgoing messages for our answering machine. Some are reverential, some humorous, and some are designed to drive telemarketers crazy... or at least enliven their days.

Since I write mainly historical fiction set in the Middle Ages or earlier, the only lyrics I ever feel compelled to include in my books are those I write myself, such as "The Caledonian Warrior's Lament" included in *Morning's Journey* and intended to be sung to the Scottish folk tune "Gloomy Winter."

I have posted a copyright notice for those lyrics in the frontmatter of *Morning's Journey* to avoid any confusion.

If you plan to include your own lyrics, poetry, art, or photos, I suggest that you attribute your copyrighted property too.

What about quoting someone else's lyrics in your book?

Attorney Kathryn Goldman covers this scenario in great depth and breadth of legalese in her article on *The Better Novel Project* blog: http://www.betternovelproject.com/blog/song-lyrics/.

The takeaway I get from her article is that unless the song is of critical importance to your story or its characters, it's best to err on the side of caution and refrain from including its lyrics in your book. Quoting lyrics—or any other type of poetry or prose, for that matter—without the express written permission of the copyright holder exposes you and your work to legal action under current copyright laws, unless the quoted work can be proven to exist in the public domain at the time of your book's publication. Furthermore, the burden of proof lies with you.

You should apply the same caution when contemplating whether to include photographs or other visual media in your book too. A common misconception, especially in the case of autographed celebrity photos, is that a photograph belongs to the subject or to the person who purchased the photo from the subject. As with lyrics, poetry, and other text, you must secure the photographer's express written permission to publish his or her work in your book or else risk serious legal consequences.

Many copyright holders are delighted to grant permission because it gives them free publicity. If you elect this route, however, make sure you give them at least three months to respond, and follow up with them if it seems to be taking longer than expected.

Sometimes, as with decades-old photographs, the copyright holder can be difficult to locate, or—as in the case of my attempting to contact someone associated with Major League Baseball to find out whether I needed permission to cite the various trademarked and service marked terms in my futuristic novel *King Arthur's Sister in Washington's Court*—they might never respond. This does not excuse you from being susceptible to copyright infringement. In those cases you would be wise to adopt my rule of thumb: when in doubt, leave it out.

2D. The Dreaded *D*-word: Crafting the Book Description

Y OU CAN STIMULATE your book sales with a tantalizing synopsis.

Please note I used the word *synopsis*, not *blurb*. There are two reasons for this.

1. I think of a "blurb" in terms of a sentence or two that has been excerpted from a larger article, such as a book review or a quote given about your book by another author.
2. THE word itself brings to mind the act of regurgitation. I would rather not have potential readers associating my book with vomit.

There. I feel much better for having gotten that off my chest; thanks.

I used to cringe at the thought of writing a short synopsis for my books—also known in traditional publishing circles as *back-cover copy* since it's included with the other elements on the back cover of a printed book.

I know I'm not alone; many authors don't feel comfortable distilling a hundred thousand words down to three hundred.

I had to get over my reluctance the hard way.

In 1997, when *Dawnflight* was acquired by Sonnet Books, a fight broke out between my editor and my literary agent, who hated the synopsis the editor had written on the grounds that it gave away too much of the plot. I could see his point. He wrote his own version, which my editor and I weren't terribly keen on because it was way too emotionless for a romance imprint. So I waded into the fray and synthesized the two versions, which did satisfy both of them and settled their argument.

The structure I prefer for back-cover copy is the tagline plus three paragraphs.

As Aristotle stated millennia ago, everything should have a beginning, a middle, and an end. This applies to back-cover copy too.

With *Dawnflight*'s first synopsis, I retained the editor's tagline-plus-three-paragraph structure. The tagline formed the beginning. The first two paragraphs—one each to introduce the heroine and hero—comprised the middle. The third and final paragraph described their mutual conundrum and its stakes. When I rereleased *Dawnflight* independently in 2013, I beefed up the concluding paragraph to highlight the book's larger scope to attract a broader audience, something for which I did not have room on the back of the original mass-market edition.

Room for the synopsis is not as big of an issue with e-books.

Amazon, for example, gives you four thousand characters in which to describe your Kindle book, and Nook grants you five thousand. Some marketing gurus will tell you that it's a great idea to use every last byte of the allotted amount, because whatever you write will factor into users' search results.

In most cases, I concur with this wisdom. The notable exception I make is in regard to my novellas and graphic novels. Since they are much shorter than my full-length novels, I've taken a page out of *The Mikado*'s playbook, and I "let the punishment fit the crime." In other words, I craft the synopsis to reflect the length of the book.

To me it just seems silly to present a book description that's almost as long as the story itself.

Although she calls it a blurb, social media manager Amy Wilkins provides more good tips about writing short synopses in this article on *Romance University*: http://romanceuniversity.org/2011/11/23/5-top-tips-for-writing-a-compelling-book-blurb-by-amy-wilkins/.

However, she does not cover one key point:

Posing a question in the synopsis is okay, but do not ask a yes-or-no question. Why?

It causes the reader to supply the answer, and then pass on buying your book. Consider the following example.

> **Book tagline:** "Can John and Marsha overcome their fears and find love in each other's arms?"
> **Me:** "Hm. This is a romance novel, so yes, that had better happen or else there's no point in reading the book."

> **Better book tagline:** "How can John and Marsha overcome their fears and find love in each other's arms?"
> **Me:** "Gee, I don't know. Maybe I ought to read a sample chapter and see if it's worth my time to find out."

Wisdom from a book PR giant

You DON'T have to be a marketing partner with the legendary BookBub to avail yourself of their "98 Book

Marketing Tips" (http://insights.bookbub.com/ book-marketing-ideas/). In case you don't have time to click through—and wade through—all ninety-eight tips, here are the two that pertain to the topic of creating your book's description:

24. Optimize your book description. BookBub's A/B testing shows that descriptions that include quotes from authors, awards, and language that caters to your audience (e.g., "If you love thrillers, don't miss this action-packed read!") have higher engagement rates.

25. Include target keywords on product pages. Narrow down a list of 5–7 keywords your audience typically searches for, then incorporate these words into your description headline, description copy, and keyword sections on each of your retailer product pages.

Studying examples from the most compelling books in your chosen genre is essential. And by "most compelling," I don't necessarily mean "best-selling" but rather, what compels you about the synopsis that entices you to learn more about that book?

I used to think that producing an excellent short synopsis was hard, but it just takes practice, and you can learn to do it too.

2E. That Thing by Which Everyone Judges Your Book (Even When the Adage Insists They Shouldn't)

T HE INJUNCTION "DON'T judge a book by its cover" was coined by an indie author who slapped together his own cover designs.

I jest, of course; the phrase has been around for decades—and the truth is that everybody judges your book by its cover. A great cover pulls in readers; a poor one can drive them away. Please trust me on this point. My books have had professionally designed covers that have existed at both ends of the pull-push reader spectrum.

2E1. What Makes for a Great Cover Design?

THE ANSWER to that question varies by genre, but the most common factors are:

- **CONTRAST.** There should be high contrast in the color scheme between the graphic images and text elements (author's name, book's title, subtitle, and other items).
- **LEGIBILITY of the thumbnail.** In forums such as Goodreads, your book's cover will live or die by its thumbnail. To test this point, create a copy of your cover file and import it into photo editing software such as Microsoft Picture Manager. Then use the "Resize" option to reduce the cover to around 80 x

120 pixels. If you can still read the title, that's great! And if your name is still legible, that's pure gravy.

- **UNIQUE manipulation of the stock model(s).** This is important because there are ever so many books on the market and vanishingly few models and poses available at the stock photo sites. Find a cover designer who will go above and beyond to make sure that your cover doesn't look like your competitors' covers.

Most of my covers have been designed by Natasha Brown of *Fostering Success* (http://www.fostering-success.com/author-services-book-covers-formatting-marketing/ebook-cover-design) and have garnered positive feedback from my readers. I'm also pleased to note that she is recognized as one of BookBub's favorite cover designers. Natasha's graphic design services are a great value for your money, and she can create other projects such as imprint logos.

Major stock photo sites include:
- **123RF** (http://www.123rf.com/)
- **Bigstock** by Shutterstock (http://www.bigstockphoto.com/)
- **Depositphotos** (http://depositphotos.com/)
- **Dreamstime** (https://www.dreamstime.com/)
- **Hot Damn Stock** (http://hotdamnstock.com/)
- **The Illustrated Romance** (https://illustratedromance.com/)
- **iStock** by Getty Images (http://www.istockphoto.com/)
- **Period Images** (http://www.periodimages.com/)
- **Razzle Dazzle Stock** (http://www.razzdazzstock.com/index)

Caution: In searching for the perfect image for your book's cover, make sure the photo is not encumbered with an *editorial* license; that type of license is only good for noncommercial use, such as on blog pages. My book layout designer at Lucky Bat Books shared a horror story with me: one of her other clients had fallen afoul of the editorial licensing issue for a book cover and was obligated to pay a $1500.00 invoice.

Do take time to read the fine print, even if you've selected a noneditorial-licensed image. Some stock photo sites stipulate limitations to the number of downloads an image can receive. Those limitations usually number ten thousand or more, but if you have a best-selling book, or if you have been lucky enough to land a BookBub promotion for it, you may need to be careful.

Most of the aforementioned stock photo sites have a checkbox so that you can exclude editorial-only licensed images from your search results. The license type you should be searching for is *royalty-free* (which, by the way, does not mean "cost free;" it just means that you pay a onetime fee to replicate and adapt the image however you wish).

2E2. E-book Cover Specifics

DETAILS RELATING to cover colors, font sizes and types, and the selection, placement, and blending of elements are largely up to the graphic designer. In general, a well-designed e-book cover will look good on all types of e-reader devices as well as on your smartphone and computer monitor. The primary difference between these devices lies in the *aspect ratio*, the value that defines the proportional relationship of an image's width to its height.

Amazon, Nook, and most of the other publishing platforms offer advice regarding which aspect ratio to apply to your book's cover prior to uploading it. This advice is geared toward sizing the cover for optimal display on the company's proprietary e-reader devices. My cover designer delivers various sizes from which to choose. In the beginning, I obediently uploaded the cover designed for the specific platform. With so many different devices on the market and with far more books in my repertoire, however, I've discovered that it's much simpler to upload the cover to all platforms at the size of 1600 x 2400 pixels, which translates to an aspect ratio of 1.5 (also expressed as 3:2). In my opinion, the overall effect is more pleasing too.

2E3. The Print Edition's Cover

IF YOUR publication plan includes releasing a print edition, then the *wraparound* ("wrap") cover is another decision you will face. Natasha Brown and most other cover designers offer this service as an add-on to commissioning an e-book cover from them, and this is the route I use most often.

Amazon's division for print edition publishing, CreateSpace (https://www.createspace.com), offers a do-it-yourself cover-creation option with several components and choices. Since I needed to print several interim copies in the process of evaluating the art placement for my fully illustrated Twain sequel, *King Arthur's Sister in Washington's Court*, and its spine thickness changed each time more art was inserted, I used CreateSpace's cover creator to take the e-book image and marry it with a coordinating solid color to form the spine and back cover. This option also permits insertion of an author photo or other image on the back; I placed a different illustration on the back cover of each interim copy so that I could keep track of the different versions during the development process.

Although I have issues with CreateSpace's print quality, especially with regard to their cover-printing process, the fact that I can upload all the interiors and cover changes I wish at no additional charge is a fantastic deal not yet matched by IngramSpark (http://www.ingram-spark.com/), my print-on-demand company of choice.

I have not yet had an opportunity to test drive the beta version of Amazon's KDP Print software, though I imagine it accesses the same cover-creation options offered by CreateSpace.

Most print-on-demand service providers offer you the choice of glossy or matte cover stock. I prefer the matte for most of my fiction and nonfiction because it looks more professional and garners greater positive response from my readers. That said, the glossy stock lends itself to certain genres like satire, or topics such as how-to manuals. I have glossy covers on my graphic novels.

Regardless of how you produce your wrap cover, placing the book's short synopsis on the back cover is essential. My husband refuses to buy any book that features a collection of accolades on the back, with no description of the story, and I know he's not alone in this preference. Space permitting, I include one quote, but only after ensuring that the synopsis is prominently displayed.

2E4. The Audiobook Cover

THE THIRD major cover type is the audiobook cover, which
has its own rules and requirements. The Amazon business unit devoted to audiobook production, Audiobook
Creation eXchange, requires that covers be sized no
smaller than 2400 x 2400 pixels. The full set of cover
requirements may be viewed on this page: http://audi-
ble-acx.custhelp.com/app/answers/detail/a_id/6654/
kw/cover.

I've seen many audiobooks whose covers appear to
be the result of taking the e-book cover and padding the
canvas to 2400x2400 pixels with a neutral background
such as black or gray. While technically this passes ACX's
sizing requirements, it looks amateurish, which you want
to avoid at all costs.

I suggest approaching your cover designer to create
a separate version for your audiobook; chances are good
that she or he will charge you only a modest fee to do
so. Another approach would be to negotiate the cost of
the audiobook cover at the same time, if your publication plan already includes producing both editions. Many
graphic designers will give you a price break for bundling
the work in this manner. This approach allows them to
plan for the alternate format, which usually results in a
more harmonious look for the two editions.

2F. Everything You Want to Know About E-book and Print Book Layouts...*

*...but were afraid to ask

So, you've written your Great [insert_your_national-ity_here] Masterpiece, edited it to within an inch of its life, submitted it to an editor so that she or he can edit it to within a micrometer of its life (*please* invest in professional editing, for the love of All That Is Holy)... and now what?

3. Formatting it for publication, of course.

There are many companies that offer formatting services, and they charge varying rates. Unless you can code your own e-books (as I do), or you can create your own print book layouts (as I have learned to do), perform a search on "book formatting services" and then pick your poison, so to speak.

Some "poisons" are more lethal to the pocketbook than others, and your mileage may vary with regard to the output quality too.

In general, your best value will be to select a company that charges an up-front fee for services, *not* a fee plus a percentage of your royalties. To charge you a percentage on sales is patently absurd, because once the work is completed, the service provider adds no more value to your work and therefore does not deserve to receive an ongoing percentage from it. Period.

Such a policy knelled the beginning of the end between

me and my ex-literary agent, who was trying to hedge his bets by publishing his clients' unsold manuscripts. If your literary agent has started such a side business, beware. All that practice does is line his or her pockets at the expense of performing his or her contracted job for you. Exclamation point.

The book service provider I have relied upon for several years is Lucky Bat Books (http://www.luckybat-books.com/). They offer a wide range of author services, including cover design and marketing, as well as e-book and print book layout. Their prices are very reasonable, they are a joy to work with, and I get nothing for sending you their way; I'm just very happy with the quality of their work. They do not charge a percentage of your sales.

Bottom line: do not select any book services provider that charges you a percentage of your book's sales over and above what you have paid up front for the work, be it cover design, interior layout, editing, e-book formatting and distribution, or promotion.

Books-A-Million has hopped onto the book-formatting bandwagon, with the added—if pricey—option of distributing your book to BAM stores. For full details, visit BAM! Publish: http://www.bampublish.com/pricing/.

I realize that not everyone can afford to lay out the huge chunk of change required for professional services, but as a former software engineer who cut her programming teeth, decades ago, on conversion software, I am here to beg you *not* to rely on the Word-to-EPUB or Word-to-PDF software offered by such companies as Smashwords and CreateSpace. I have seen other authors' books generated by these programs, and they are—shall I say?—less than ideal.

At least Smashwords is honest in nicknaming its program the "Meat Grinder."

I ran a test to export an EPUB e-book file from a print layout that I had created using Adobe InDesign document layout software, and its quality left a lot to be desired too.

My recommendation is to set up crowdfunding for your book rather than relying on these cheap-but-less-than-optimal conversion options.

The book layout process I follow varies by edition type, e-book versus print.

2F1. E-book Layout Process

The primary rule you must remember about e-book coding is that **an e-book is not a print book**. Do not get hung up on trying to control your audience's digital reading experience down to the gnat's eyebrow by locking in font types and text sizes. The fact is that a user may elect to change those parameters on the fly, so the more controls you impose upon your e-book, the greater the risk that some user's setting might make your book look terrible, thereby causing him or her to never buy another of your books.

One such example is the use of drop caps. They look cool in a print book, but their display can be inconsistent across different e-reader devices. Although I know how to code drop caps in an e-book, I abandoned the practice years ago in favor of decorating the opening words of chapters and scenes by removing the first paragraph's indentation and altering the relative sizes of the first three or two words, respectively. As an old-school programmer, I adhere to the philosophy of making my e-books as device-independent as possible.

An e-book (EPUB) file is a rigidly formatted ZIP file, and HTML is its source language. I'm not a CSS expert; a mentor shared her e-book template with me years ago, and I've been tweaking it ever since. For quick answers and to look up the latest HTML code sets, I rely upon the website *HTML Dog* (http://www.htmldog.com/).

A personal bugaboo of mine deserving mention is the use of italics, which must be designated with <i></i> tags surrounding the affected text in the e-book's HTML file. Sometimes the use of italics is required, as with book titles. Every time you apply text decoration, you introduce a mental speed bump into the human reading process. Therefore, I urge you to treat italics as you would season your food with salt. A pinch too much, perhaps one italicized word per chapter, can detract from the sensory experience and potentially throw your reader out of the story each time. Way too much—as in, more than once per scene unless you're using that technique to delineate a dream or flashback—and you risk losing that reader forever.

Something else to bear in mind is that you must insert scene-break graphics or text between each scene, since breaks can occur at any point on the screen as the result of a user's personal preferences for text size. I use small graphics files in most of my books, and I size them to a height of 150 pixels for chapters and one hundred pixels for scenes. If both dimensions are less than one hundred, then it's very difficult for a user to click on a graphic to enlarge it. Be aware that KDP will shrink your graphics to about half the original size, so don't be dismayed if the MOBI display looks different than the EPUB edition the Nook-using segment of your audience will purchase.

In general, if the margins, indentation, line spacing,

graphics sizes, and relative font sizing parameters you have chosen yield a pleasing result for you, then your readers ought to find the resulting e-book display pleasing too.

My e-book production steps:

1. I code the HTML, including setting up CSS templates for margins, line spacing, indentations, and other display attributes.

2. To test the book's format prior to conversion, I read it in a browser window sized to approximate the aspect ratio of the average e-reader device. This also gives me another avenue for spotting last-minute typos and items to wordsmith.

3. ONCE I'm happy with how the HTML file looks in a browser window, I import the code, the cover, and *metadata* into Calibre (http://calibre-ebook.com/) free library-management software. Metadata is literally anything you wish to define about your book. Specific metadata tags that import into predefined fields in Calibre include:
    *   AUTHOR
    *   SERIES
    *   TAGS (i.e., keywords)
    *   PUBLISHER

    I also code the book's description in the metadata section so it's available for my reference.

4. THEN I use Calibre to convert the HTML file to EPUB. Calibre offers more than a dozen output formats, but the two I use most often are EPUB and MOBI (primarily for reviewers who have the ability to side-load the MOBI file into their Kindle devices).

5. AT this point I check the EPUB file in as many e-reader emulators as I can. Calibre offers its own e-reader

emulator; on my laptop, clicking on the MOBI version imports it into my Kindle-for-PC application, and if I upload the EPUB file to my Android phone, I can import it into my Nook-for-Android app.

6. ONCE I am satisfied with the result on as many platforms as possible, I run the EPUB file through EPUBCheck (http://validator.idpf.org/), a free online validation tool created by the International Digital Publishing Forum. E-tailers such as Amazon and Smashwords also run your submitted EPUB file through EPUBCheck, but it's best for you to do this first and avoid any unpleasant surprises. Smashwords sometimes will report an "error" on the website's dashboard, only to turn around and email you the happy news that your file passed their internal test, something you already knew if you ran EPUBCheck ahead of time.

7. IF EPUBCheck has reported any errors, I fix them and revalidate. The biggest "gotcha," if you have been otherwise careful in your coding, is to have referenced image filenames that include embedded spaces, a practice that's allowed on Microsoft computers but not on Apple or Unix machines. EPUBCheck flags this as a warning, but even warning messages will cause your submission to be rejected by Amazon, et al.

8. ONCE you have an error-free and warning-free EPUB file, you may upload it for publication on all your chosen platforms. When updating existing titles, my convention is to begin with Smashwords, then progress to the other vendors, and end with Amazon so that I'm not tempted to compromise my version control by skipping the less profitable accounts. Amazon will also accept a MOBI file for uploading to KDP.

2F2. Print Book Layout Process

AN INTERIOR layout for a print book is developed as a series of spreads. A *spread* is a pair of pages representing an open book.

The only technical requirements imposed upon print books are that the spread's outside margins must be at least 0.25", and the inside (a.k.a. *gutter*) margins must be sized to accommodate the book's spine thickness, which is dictated by page count. The thicker the book, the wider the gutter margin. CreateSpace offers margin sizing guidelines in relation to your book's page count on this page: https://www.createspace.com/Products/Book/InteriorPDF.jsp.

All other margin settings, font types and sizing, indentation, line spacing, page numbering styles and placement, and other parameters may be chosen at the discretion of the layout designer, though books aimed at teens and younger audiences generally require wider margins and line spacing, and larger and simpler fonts.

For print books that don't have a lot of complicated interior art insertion:

1. I import the manuscript into Adobe InDesign, the de facto standard document-layout software for the publishing industry.
2. I tweak the layout—defining custom paragraph styles, drop cap styles, and so forth—until it all looks good, right, and salutary... and everything lines up across each spread. If you have no scene-break graphics to insert, then this step is almost a no-brainer. I embed graphics below chapter headings and as scene breaks, so this step can be time-consuming for me, and it's

more cost effective for me to do it myself. Also, the "spreads" PDF output option of InDesign is an economical way to produce a printed advance reader copy, especially if you have access to a duplex printer.

3. I export the finished layout to a press-ready PDF file in "pages" (one book page per PDF page) form. This is the required format for submitting your interior print layout to CreateSpace and IngramSpark.

I don't know InDesign well enough yet to execute complicated layouts, which is why I am still happy to employ Lucky Bat Books for titles such as the fully illustrated—and award-winning—hardcover and paperback editions of *King Arthur's Sister in Washington's Court*.

CreateSpace's Interior Reviewer software allows you to upload your Word DOC or RTF file, and it will generate the PDF file representing the book's interior for you (source https://www.createspace.com/Tools/InteriorReviewer.jsp). I never intend to use this feature, however, because of my aforementioned aversion to book-conversion software.

If you want to try developing your own book layouts but don't know where to start, select a book in your genre whose layout you admire and emulate its margins and other parameters. Having a printer's ruler that gives measures in picas and points in addition to millimeters and inches is a definite plus.

Regarding paper selection: Most print-on-demand service providers offer you the choice of publishing your book on creme or white paper. That's primarily an aesthetic choice, though creme paper is slightly thicker and heavier than white and will therefore be a bit more expensive in terms of both printing and shipping costs.

2G. The Audiobook, or "Friends, Romans, Countrymen..."

WITH A MANUSCRIPT sold to a traditional publisher such as Simon & Schuster or HarperCollins, the author usually must sell all rights—including the right to produce ancillary editions such as the audiobook—and then sit around hoping and praying that the mass-market paperback does well enough to convince the publisher to publish the novel in other formats.

Not so in this day and age of independent publishing, thank heaven.

In 1997, when the first edition of *Dawnflight* was having its contract negotiated with Simon & Schuster, their boilerplate stipulated the purchase of a lot of rights, including foreign translations and the production of an audiobook edition. The prospect of seeing my work in those other formats was exciting. However, Simon & Schuster never exploited those rights, so when the 1999 mass-market paperback edition went out of print in 2004, the ancillary rights reverted to me as well.

The novel in all formats lay fallow until 2012, when I decided to overhaul it and release it as an official second edition in print as well as e-book. My e-book coding mentor introduced me to the unique joys of audiobook production using Amazon's ACX audiobook production platform, and although I am aware of other audiobook production services, I have never felt the need to take my audiobooks anywhere else.

2G1. The ACX Audiobook Production Process

1. A book's *rights holder*—author or publisher—visits the ACX website (http://www.acx.com/) and signs in with his or her existing Amazon account.
2. ONCE logged in, "claim" the book using ACX's "Add Your Title" function (top right corner of window). This performs a search of the Amazon product catalog to retrieve available editions.
3. STIPULATE whether the audiobook will be self-narrated.
4. FILL out all the requisite information about the title, including:
   - **PRODUCTION payment type:** You can choose *royalty share* (50-50 split of net royalties paid to rights holder and producer, meaning the producer bears all risk for production), or pay some agreed-upon amount upon completion of the project (i.e., the rights holder bears all the risk). In this context, *producer* refers to the person or production company responsible for creating the finished audiobook edition. ACX sometimes will agree to pay the producer a fee even though the rights holder has stipulated a royalty-share contract; this happened for my e-book coding mentor with her first audiobook but not for any of my titles thus far, and of course it's not applicable for self-narrated titles.
   - **DISTRIBUTION:** Choose either *exclusive* (distribution to Audible, Amazon, and iTunes only, which yields a 40 percent net royalty for the title), or

nonexclusive (distribution to Audible, Amazon, iTunes, and anywhere else of the rights holder's choosing at a 25 percent net royalty). The 40 percent or 25 percent amount is what is split with the producer in a royalty-share production agreement.

IF the audiobook is not to be self-narrated, other parameters such as the type of voice desired (male or female, age, narration style, accent, and other vocal attributes) may be specified, in addition to the book's genre and other details.

5. UPLOAD an audition script (or not, if you're narrating your own title, and skip the next step too). The ideal audition script will feature a key scene from your book that includes dialogue for the main character(s) so that you can evaluate the prospective narrator's emotional and vocal range. The audition script should be no more than 750 words (a maximum reading time of about five minutes). If you upload a longer script, don't be surprised if the candidate doesn't read it all. In the comments section, do specify details such as the characters' ages and accents and expected pronunciation of unusual names or words to give candidates the best chance of recording a great audition for you.

6. EITHER wait for a producer to submit an audition, or search for suitable producers and contact them using ACX's messaging system. The latter entails listening to posted clips and can be very time-consuming. I have done the proactive approach for only two producers, and neither of them answered me. If you have had luck with this approach, drop me a line to let me

know!

7. ONCE the rights holder receives an acceptable audition (or not, if self-narrating), then the process of recording and approving audiobook chapters begins. If you're not doing your own recording, this phase consists of waiting for the producer to upload a new segment, listening to the segment, and providing feedback. The length of this phase is usually a direct correlation to the length of the source material, although I once had to officially cease production on a project because the producer fell ill and couldn't complete it.

   For all of my completed projects, I elected to manage them on a chapter-by-chapter basis, and I have developed a spreadsheet to identify specific problem areas as well as to communicate positive feedback. Like any type of artist, most vocal artists take great pride in their work and welcome feedback so that both parties are happy with the production.

   I do not recommend waiting to listen to the producer's work until after all files have been delivered because of the sheer amount and variety of issues that can crop up, some of which may impact the rest of the production. It is far better for everyone involved to keep on top of the process at every step along the way.

8. UPON final approval of all chapters, and uploading of the cover art and retail sample (a three- to five-minute excerpt), the rights holder (and producer, if they are in a royalty-share agreement) waits for ACX to perform an internal quality-control audit of the audiobook.

For the 2013 editions of *Dawnflight* and *The Color*

of Vengeance, the internal ACX audit took about a month between my acceptance of the files and ACX's release of the audiobooks into retail channels.

With *The Challenge*, I elected to enter into a per-finished-hour payment agreement (rather than royalty share; see below for explanation) with an ACX-certified producer, and the internal audit was completed in less than two weeks—with the US Thanksgiving holiday smack in the middle. Whether this speed increase was due to hiring a certified producer or not, I cannot be certain, but obviously it didn't hurt. And I scored a few extras, such as special voice modulation effects, in the bargain.

9. WAIT another week or so for the title to cross-populate into Amazon and iTunes catalogs, and begin the manual distribution process to other sites such as CD Baby (http://members.cdbaby.com/faq.aspx) if you've chosen nonexclusive distribution.

2G2. Choosing the Right Producer for Your Audiobook

IF YOU have a best-selling title, you want to delve into crowdfunding, or you are otherwise wealthy enough to drop five thousand dollars or more on paying someone else to produce your audiobook, you can investigate the high-end independent producers mentioned in *BookLife* (http://booklife.com/publish/audio/06/29/2015/the-indie-authors-guide-to-diy-audiobooks.html), the news outlet produced by *Publishers Weekly* for independent authors.

Otherwise, decide upon the type of voice you're looking for, establish your ACX budget, and hope for the best.

Paying for production entails a unit called the *finished hour*. For planning purposes when setting up your book to receive auditions, ACX estimates one finished hour to be 9,300 words of text.

Once the book is recorded and uploaded to ACX, then the actual production cost is calculated to be the sum total in hours and minutes of all files multiplied by the agreed-upon per-finished-hour rate. Producers with a presence in ACX stipulate their minimum accepted PFH rate, though it may be open to negotiation. If you do elect to negotiate, whether you're a rights holder or a producer, keep in mind that ACX's offer-rejection letter sent to the other party may sound final but really isn't, and submit (or accept, if you're the producer) a new offer. Positive communication between the rights holder and prospective producer is crucial.

My 135,000-word manuscript for *Dawnflight* was estimated to be 14.5 finished hours... and the final production weighed in at 17.7 hours. If I had hired an ACX-certified producer for that project, at $200.00 per finished hour (a typical rate for that level of production experience), I'd have been on the hook to pay more than $3,500.00.

That is the kind of math to be aware of when making your audiobook title setup decisions. Producers registered within ACX (whether certified or not) may elect to be paid in the following PFH increments: $0–$50, $50–$100, $100–$200, $200–$400, and $400–$1000. One thousand dollars per finished hour will usually get you a team of male and female voice artists, musical interludes, sound effects, and the whole truckload of enchiladas. The $0–$50 end will yield a basic production, perhaps by someone just starting out in the narration business; in that case, you're probably better off stipulating the royalty-share production arrangement and seeing if you can attract a producer with a higher experience level.

An option that's priced competitively with ACX's PFH pricing model is Booktrack (https://promo.booktrack.com/self-publish), which you can commission to create a soundtrack of your book complete with royalty-free music and sound effects. However, a distinct drawback is that Booktrack soundtracks are marketed only to Booktrack subscribers. The soundtracks use synchronization tools available from the Google Play and iTunes apps stores, but it's up to you to inform your audience about where to find your book's soundtrack and how to synchronize it with Google Play or iTunes.

2G3. Getting Audiobook Reviews

If you think it's hard to get your e-book reviewed (refer to the "Marketing" chapter for more thoughts on that topic), just wait till you have an audiobook to promote. To get you started, here are a few sites to contact:

- **Audiobook Fans** http://www.audiobookfans.com/review-policy/
- **Audiobook Jukebox** http://audiobookjukebox.squarespace.com/solid-gold-reviewer-program/. You don't have to distribute your Audible download codes if your audiobook is listed here, which is a fabulous deal. The downside is that your audiobook remains available to reviewers for a limited time of your choosing, up to six months. Check their submission policy if you write erotica; as of this writing, they

do not accept that genre. Furthermore, they distribute a maximum of five review copies per title per listing period, so you cannot use this site for scheduling an audiobook review blog tour.

- **AUDIOBOOK Review** http://audiobookreviewer.com/review-policy/ (sci-fi/fantasy only)
- **BOOKS for Ears** http://booksforears.com/contact-us/ (no review submission policy; just contact them with your query)

3. PRESENTING

B Y *PRESENTING* I don't necessarily mean getting up in front of a room full of people to deliver a talk about your book or a related topic, though public speaking is touched upon in this chapter. I refer instead to the general process of establishing and managing the means by which your books—and, indeed, yourself—are perceived by your readers.

3A. Author Branding, or "How Do I Rope in More Readers?"

THERE'S ALL KINDS of advice online regarding how any entrepreneur can establish a clear branding message, but the best comment about the topic that I've read was posted by *She Owns It* blog contributor Lorea Sample:

> Push past the fears of rejection, acceptance, and being misunderstood and flow in your being. **Embrace and become resolute in all of your you-ness and your branding and messaging will flow.** Like they say, "Your Vibe Attracts Your Tribe." Have a clear and consistent vibe and your tribe will understand and consistently be attracted to you. (**emphasis** mine; read the full article here: http://sheownsit.com/30912-2/)

This struck a chord with me because fears of rejection and being misunderstood haunt me as an author, and I have to imagine that I'm not alone in this feeling.

Once you have established your branding, you need to do all you can to expand it.

Authors primarily establish their branding by the books they write, genre (for fiction) or topic (for nonfiction), and quality. Most authors have no trouble deciding what they want to write, and the issue of assessing and improving upon a written work's quality is an entire book in itself.

After an author has established his or her brand, its

refinement is a three-step process:

1. **DETERMINE your audience.** If you write nonfiction, chances are you are already aware of your intended audience and won't try to, for example, market a dentistry book to medical doctors. Audience determination for fiction is a little more involved. Ask yourself what sort of person will be attracted by the age, sex, personality, and values of your protagonist. It's possible for your characters and their situations to appeal to readers residing in different demographics; for example, many adults love to read young adult titles. Decide upon your primary audience first, and be prepared to market to secondary audiences in future campaigns.

2. **LEARN what your audience prefers.** Study other authors' books in your chosen genre or field. If, for example, you want to write "sweet" romance, you shouldn't be using language that appeals to erotica readers. It's okay to experiment with pushing boundaries in terms of language or scenarios, but be prepared for a backlash in reviews and rankings if enough of your target audience believes you've gone too far.

3. **APPEAL to your audience.** Write your author bio and book's description in a manner that reflects the book itself or its main character. On social media platforms, share pictures, memes, quotes, and other content that suggest you, your protagonist, or your book without being directly related. Engage with bloggers, followers, and other individuals in a friendly and welcoming manner without hitting them with a barrage of "buy my book" pleas.

A note about memes: I used GIFCreator (http://gif-creator.me/), a free tool that allows the creation of animated memes using your own photos and other images, to create the animated meme for *Kings* displayed in the "About the Author" section of the e-book edition. If you read this book on your Kindle device or app, however, you will see only the last frame of the animation because KDP blocks the inclusion of all types of moving images, including embedded YouTube videos, during its conversion process.

I've been doing a lot of mentoring of various author-friends, and an email exchange with one of them inspired further thoughts about author branding.

The conversation started when I was preparing a post to feature one of her books on *The Maze*. I usually try to check all the author's links, and when I got to the link she'd provided for Google+, I noticed that she had garnered more than nine followers, the minimum required to customize her G+ link, but hadn't yet done so.

I suggested that she check into it as yet another way to expand her author brand.

Her response, after setting up her new G+ link, was: "How do you use that to expand your brand?"

I'm so glad she asked, because this is a topic that is becoming more crucial to authors wanting to claw their way to the surface of the ocean of available books in order for their work to be noticed.

Common wisdom states that it takes *at least* seven mentions of an advertisement before a customer decides to purchase the product. Books are increasingly being perceived as a commodity while not being, strictly speaking, a necessity for basic living. So customers require lot more convincing before they'll part with their hard earned cash.

Anywhere in Social Media Land (Tumblr, Reddit, and so on) that you can claim your name will expand your brand, provided that you are active—and interactive—on those sites. Top-notch social media promotion is quite literally a full-time job, so you must choose the platforms where you plan to be most active if you want to stand a prayer of getting any actual writing done too.

I have chosen the following, in this order:

- Twitter (https://twitter.com/KimHeadlee)
- Facebook (https://www.facebook.com/kim.headlee)
- Google+ (https://plus.google.com/+KimHeadlee)
- Pinterest (http://www.pinterest.com/kimheadlee/)
- YouTube (http://www.youtube.com/user/gyanhu-mara)
- Goodreads (http://www.goodreads.com/author/show/845537.Kim_Headlee)

That said, Facebook, G+, and Pinterest are tied for how much involvement I do on those platforms. I use Facebook far more for keeping up with my kids and face-to-face friends than for promotion. On my YouTube channel I upload my book trailers and the occasional video I create myself, so there's not a lot of regular action there. I do have a Tumblr account, but only because I needed to have one in order to read a review of one of my books that someone had posted on that platform.

Google+ has been handy for sharing my blog posts as well as review posts of my books on other blogs. I love that I can choose to cross-post Pinterest pins to Twitter

Facebook on a pin-by-pin basis. I also have found ̣est to be invaluable for graphic collaboration with ̣tists I have hired for one reason or another; devel- ̣nent of the graphic novel edition of *The Challenge* is ̣ne project du jour for me.

Thanks to a reminder by author Alethea Kontis at MarsCon 2016, where we were both panelists, I have now claimed my username at Instagram (https://www.instagram.com/kimheadlee/), Reddit (https://www.reddit.com/user/KimHeadlee/), and other places.

Expanding your brand means getting your name—and your you-ness—out there in as diverse a way possible, because you never know who's going to see what when.

3B. Pen Names, or "An Author by Any Other Name…"

Close your books and grab your pens, class. Here is your pop quiz for the day.

Who was/is…?

- Mark Twain
- George Sand
- CJ Cherryh
- Kimberly Iverson

Just about everyone with decent grades in high school English should know that Mark Twain is the most famous pen name of several used by Samuel Langhorne Clemens.

Bonus points if you knew (or were able to look up) that George Sand was born Amantine-Lucile-Aurore Dupin, and that Carolyn Janice Cherry went by her initials and stuck an *h* onto the end of her name so that her science fiction novels didn't appear to be written by a romance author.

Mega bonus points if you figured out that "Kimberly Iverson" is me.

There many reasons to establish a pseudonym, some relevant to this day and age, such as Clemens's intent to prevent any potential literary backlash from affecting his brother Orion's political career. Other reasons—for example, a woman inventing a man's name because authors were predominantly men, as in the cases of Dupin and

Cherry—perhaps not so much. I even see men's names on erotica romance these days.

Establishing a pseudonym, once you've invented one you like that enhances your brand and you have performed enough research to determine that no one else is using it, is as easy as typing it on your book's title page.

Managing one or more pseudonyms, however, is the real trick.

An article written by Derek Haines (http://www.derekhaines.ch/vandal/2012/04/publishing-using-a-pen-name/) on his blog discusses doing this within KDP and is a good starting point.

What he doesn't cover is that you can establish multiple author pages on retail and book-discussion forums such as Amazon, Goodreads, and LibraryThing.

When it came time for my literary agent to shop around the first edition of my novel *Liberty* in 2003, he advised that I submit it under a pseudonym since *Dawnflight* hadn't been an overnight sensation. I chose Kimberly Iverson, and my agent found an editor at HQN Books who was willing to take a chance on a "first time" author with the project. When she learned that I had published with Simon & Schuster just a few years earlier, it made *Liberty* all the easier to sell to her management.

I already had a "Kim Headlee" author page on Amazon (http://Author.to/Kim_Headlee_Amazon_page), so I created one for "Kimberly Iverson" (https://www.amazon.com/Kimberly-Iverson/e/B001JRZCGU/) tied to a different email address to delineate the two accounts in their system. Simple as that.

Once I started self-publishing under a blend of both names, "Kim Iverson Headlee," I added the other permutations to each of the books' contributor fields in the metadata so that fans of "Kim Headlee," "Kimberly Iverson," or "Kim Iverson Headlee" can find all my books using whichever author search parameters they employ.

Having one or more books in print automatically gets the author's name established in discussion forums such as Goodreads. In my case, I had to contact a super librarian in the Goodreads Librarians Group to sort out the merging of my "Kim Headlee" and "Kimberly Iverson" author profiles into "Kim Iverson Headlee." Goodreads super librarians are very supportive and helpful, and they will also advise when and how to make changes for yourself.

I recommend that all authors join the Goodreads Librarians Group (https://www.goodreads.com/group/show/220-goodreads-librarians-group), because you never know when you'll need extra information or when some glitch or special request might pop up that you cannot correct on your own.

I chose to merge my various pen names for several reasons, not the least of which being that it's easier to manage one author page per platform than three. Whether you take this approach or not is up to you, but your sanity may thank you if you do.

3C. On Being a Professional Writer, or "Who Let *That* Dog Out?"

A COMMENT I heard often in 1997 after landing my first New York publishing contract was "Congratulations; you're running with the big dogs now!" It was a good thing that occurred before Baha Men released their hit single or I might have driven my first fans crazy serenading them with the famous refrain... and I would have lost major points for professionalism.

Although the concept of the "lonely writer's garret" still carries a certain romantic flair, once a writer has transitioned into preparing to make money off his or her words, he or she becomes a professional writer.

But what does that mean, exactly?

Writers being creative beings, this can mean a number of different things in terms of personal appearance, behavior, and habits. For the writer who wishes to be perceived as a professional, these aspects center upon various demonstrations of common courtesy... the exercise of which seems to be eroding in this day and age of Internet anonymity.

Opportunities for an author's professionalism to shine include correspondence, deadlines, and personal appearances.

3C1. Correspondence

As A professional writer, you should always remain mindful of how you are perceived by your audience, not only in the content of your books or articles but in everyday correspondence tasks. This applies to email, text, chatting, and "earthmail" interactions with:

- **LITERARY agents, editors, cover and interior-layout designers, promotional companies, accountants, and other service personnel.** This includes all individuals and companies, whether prospective or contracted.
- **BOOKSELLERS and other event organizers**, both before the event and in giving thanks afterward. Expressing appreciation can be the fastest way to earn a return invitation.
- **BOOK bloggers and other reviewers**, when asking for reviews as well as in optionally expressing thanks for a helpful review. Never engage a reviewer if you are in any way dissatisfied with the review. I discuss that advice in the "Marketing" chapter, but it cannot be emphasized enough.
- **YOUR fans**—and this goes double for anything written online, even in so-called private messages. Any site can be hacked or monitored, so the best policy is to presume that nothing is private and structure your interactions accordingly.
- **ANYONE with whom you need to send follow-up correspondence** for any reason.

3C2. Deadlines

AH, THE other dreaded *d*-word besides the book description. For journalists, deadlines are most often perceived as just a means of structuring one's workday. For everyone else, especially those of us who write book-length fiction or nonfiction, adhering to content delivery deadlines that are established by another party such as a publisher can be problematical at best. And yet delivering a completed manuscript on time will set you apart from the madding crowd of authors who play fast and loose with their time and with their editor's or publisher's patience.

3C3. Personal Appearances

THERE EXIST countless opportunities to present yourself as a professional writer in public.

- **ONLINE.** I have already covered fan interactions; here I refer to things such as the random tweets, retweets, pictures, videos, and status updates that you choose to share to your sundry social media platforms. As you decide upon your online persona, make sure that it jives with what you write, for that persona will become a part of your author brand. And then tweet/ retweet/share accordingly. For example, if you write Christian fiction, I would advise against saying anything in a tweet that you wouldn't say in church.
- **BOOK vending and signings at bookstores and conferences.** Your in-person persona should also jive (or at least not conflict) with what you write. On the other hand, if you write about serial killers, you might wish to think twice about acting like one in public. You can get a lot of mileage from being courteous, respectful, and appreciative of customers, noncustomers, and event hosts, regardless of what type of books you write. Keep in mind that you are competing for readers, some of whom may

be offended and turned off from your books if you act rude, superior, or condescending in person.

When in doubt, recall the mantra spouted by the Penguins of Madagascar: "Just smile and wave, boys, smile and wave."

- **WRITERS' conferences.** If you're a member of the Romance Writers of America, I don't need to tell you how to present yourself as a professional in this type of venue. You know already—or you should. Although I haven't attended an RWA national conference in several years, I can pretty much imagine what the most recent one looked like: out of two thousand attendees, 1,942 were power-suited women (whether publishers, editors, literary agents, or authors), fifty-five were similarly attired men, and the remaining three were newbie women authors who didn't receive the dress code memo, showed up in blue jeans and an "I [heart] My Book Boyfriend" T-shirt, and missed the entire first day of panels shopping for an emergency power suit and accessories. Okay, I jest... but barely.

  The dress code memos will of course vary by genre. At a typical World Fantasy Convention you'll see no shortage of suits, but very few of those will be draped over authors, who sport pretty much whatever tickles their fancy, short of character costumes. Although I haven't attended a WFC since the debut of the first edition of *Dawnflight* in 1999, I have it on excellent authority that a few steampunk outfits show up here and there, so if that's your chosen genre, then by all means go for it.

- **THE grocery store.** The what? Yes, there is always the

possibility that you could be recognized in a chance public encounter, so your appearance and behavior choices matter there too.

As I always advised my kids as they were growing up, no one will ever fault you for being polite, gracious, appreciative, respectful, and kind. The people you impress with your professionalism may remember those choices and become extra supportive of you and your work.

3D. On Labeling Yourself a Best-Selling Author, or "It's All Fun and Games until Someone Gets Caught"

EARLY ON AUGUST 10, 2015, my young adult paranormal medieval romance novel *Snow in July* hit the top spot in the category of paid Kindle teen and young adult historical romances. It got as high as number two in teen historical romance books (all formats) and number twenty-four in teen paranormal romance that morning too. It was a lovely surprise to wake up to, and I thank everyone who downloaded the book to make it possible.

I am also grateful that I captured the screenshot when I did, because on the product page for *Snow in July*, Amazon had already reported that my book was number two in the teen and young adult historical romances Kindle category and even lower ranks for the other two. I almost didn't click through to "see the top 100" to discover the very pleasant surprise that *Snow in July* had reached number one during the night.

So my book's "best-seller" status lasted just a few hours, but the lists hadn't yet caught up to the product page. Did I rush forth and change my Twitter profile to add "best-selling author" and crank out a bunch of tweets, pins, and status updates to blare this news before everything synched?

H*ll, no.

Congratulations if this has happened to any of your books, but you shouldn't do that either.

I'm serious. Because Amazon category best-selling ranks are that fleeting, they are meaningless. Because they are meaningless, those labels in a tweet, meme, or other social media post do nothing to sway me toward buying a book unless prefaced by the phrases "*USA Today*" or "*New York Times*" ...and it's a rare day when I buy off those lists either.

I cannot count the number of times that I've noticed such a tweet, clicked through on the link, and seen the book's Amazon rank numbering in the tens of thousands, sometimes even the hundreds of thousands or millions. Do you know what that does to a "best-selling" (but not today) author's credibility in my eyes?

I'll give you three guesses, and the first two don't count.

Yes, it's an exciting accomplishment that presents a tremendous temptation to claim the Amazon category "best-selling" badge. But I'm here to beg you not to succumb. You're only hurting your branding and marketing efforts if you do.

4. MARKETING

I F ORGANIZING IS the vegetable dish, packaging is the entrée, and presenting is the gravy, now we come to the potatoes of the meal: marketing. It's the starchy glue that sticks all our efforts together and gives our books the energy boost they need to reach the next tier of sales results.

Not long ago I read something that was described as a joke, but it isn't funny to the hundreds of thousands of authors who struggle just to break even on their books:

> How do you make $100,000.00 in book sales?
> Spend $200,000.00.

I will never claim that applying the advice in this chapter will propel you into the black with regard to your book's sales—though if that happy day occurs, I trust you will tell me about it! I do hope my marketing insights can at least cut down the loss margin for you.

Marketing isn't about sales. Marketing is about building name recognition that eventually leads to sales.

In this chapter I cover many aspects of book marketing, including the promotion plan, the author's blog and newsletter, free and paid advertising options, other online promotions, book reviews, keyword development, creating permafree titles, running giveaways, digital distribution strategies, and more. A lot more. As in, about half this book. That alone should clue you in to the importance marketing plays in the business of writing.

4A. The Promotion Plan, or "We Don't Need No—Yes, We Do!"

YOU'VE PUBLISHED YOUR fabulous book, and now it's time to promote the dickens out of it, right?

Wrong.

To achieve maximum sales success—whether you are a "traditional," "independent," or "hybrid" published author—you need to formulate your promotion plan in conjunction with your publication plan (refer to the "Organizing" chapter) several months in advance of your anticipated release date. My minimum recommendation is six months, and the longer lead time you can give yourself, the better.

If the book you wish to promote is under contract with a publisher, then chances are they have developed its publication plan for you. If the title you have published with them is so hot in terms of projected sales that they feel compelled to alert FedEx of the tonnage of its global shipments, then chances are they are managing the lion's share of your promotion plan too. And, chances are, you are not reading this book.

For the rest of you, I offer the following advice, honed over the course of my two-decade hybrid publishing career, for key elements to include in your promotion plan.

4A1. The ARC

THIS IS not a geometry term, and you don't have to raid an Egyptian dig site to find one; in this context it's an acronym for advance reader copy. The ARC may be either digital or printed.

If you're traditionally published, as I was for my first two novels, you may receive a box of ARCs that your publisher printed and expects you to distribute to reviewers and local bookstores. If you need to create a printable ARC of your manuscript, I suggest converting it to a PDF file first. Either way, printed and digital ARCs need to get into reviewers' hands a minimum of three months in advance of the release date if you want reviews to be posted in conjunction with your book's release. But do your homework and pay attention to the fine print. Some review organizations, such as Publisher's Weekly, require a six-month lead time.

Note: If you're releasing your book yourself, *Publishers Weekly*'s site for independent authors, *BookLife* (http://booklife.com/), will not accept ARCs in any format prior to the release date. The good news is that you can save on postage by submitting a camera-ready PDF representing the actual print edition published by your print-on-demand printer such as CreateSpace or IngramSpark.

4A2. Media Kit Overview

THE MEDIA kit for your book isn't what it used to be, and I delve into that in greater detail later in the chapter. Suffice it to say that you need to factor the media kit into your promotion plan. I recommend keeping a separate s, and keep them updated

l links become known.

ew

opic that I have devoted
this chapter. But for the
lan, especially if you are
landed a contract or has
xpanding your networks
ait until after the book's
release to begin that process. Unless you're lucky enough to have a blockbuster on your hands, you'll find it difficult to gain any sort of sales traction that way.

For the average author, it takes between one and two years to develop a respectable following on any of the major platforms. This can be accelerated by conducting more personal interaction, but the tradeoff is the time investment—time that could be better spent writing and polishing your book.

4A4. Blog Tours, Facebook Parties, and the Like

IF YOU'RE comfortable—or wish to try—interacting online with people you haven't met in person, these events should be an integral part of your promotion plan whether you are publishing independently or not. Every event, even the ever-popular cover reveals, should be scheduled with either preordering or purchasing your book in mind. If you are releasing your book exclusively on Kindle, coordinate the virtual tour or party with either a Countdown Deal (https://kdp.amazon.com/help?topicId=A3288N75MH14B8) or Free Book Promotion (https://kdp.amazon.com/help?topicId=A34IQ0W14Z-KXM9) to maximize interest in your release. If you are soliciting reviews for the event, schedule it *at least* four months in advance to give reviewers as much time as possible to read your book.

Note: Reviews cannot be posted on Amazon while a book exists in the preorder phase, so if you're trying to line up reviews to be posted right away, schedule your event at least a day or two after your book's release to give time for its product pages to go live worldwide. Bloggers are busy people too, so if they visit your book's product page but cannot post their reviews, they might not return to do so at a later date.

Hot tip for your Amazon book links: You can set up free links to all editions of your books—e-books, print editions, and audiobooks—that are sold in the Amazon product catalog that automatically click through to Amazon in the reader's home country—and you can specify your Amazon affiliate ID for each country where you have one—on BookLinker (http://booklinker.net/). The BookLinker folks have redesigned their site since I wrote my original blog post on the topic; it now includes a means to delete a link if you've made a mistake or have removed a book from publication. With BookLinker you can also set up a worldwide link to your Amazon author page, and the per-country click statistics are fascinating.

Even hotter tip, for *all* your e-book links: You don't have to be a Draft2Digital author to avail yourself of their universal link creation service offered by sister site Books2Read (https://books2read.com/faq/author/). It's free, and a nice benefit is they allow the user to specify affiliate ID tags for Google Play, the iBooks Store, Barnes

& Noble, and other e-tailers in addition to Amazon. The software scans for links to your book all across cyber-space, including European sites such as Thalia.de and 24Symbols. Another neat trick is that it allows you to customize the link to turn off the application of affiliate IDs and/or to direct the visitor to a specific store. The latter is helpful when embedding the link in an e-book or anywhere else where specification of affiliate IDs or universal links is not permitted.

I prefer to pay companies such as Magic of Books (http://magicofbookspromo.blogspot.com/p/welcome-to-magic-of-books-promotions.html) and Goddess Fish (http://www.goddessfish.com/services/) for coordi-nating my books' **blog tours**. A Google search will turn up dozens more, and they charge varying amounts, up to several hundred dollars per tour. If you would rather assemble your own blog tour and need advice, please visit the guest post on *The Maze* contributed by author Liza O'Connor: http://kimiversonheadlee.blogspot.com/2015/10/the-business-of-writing-diy-blog-tours.html.

Note: Goddess Fish offers graphic design (including book covers) and other prepublication services in addi-tion to promotional services. I have no experience with this aspect of their business and thus can only comment upon its existence.

I've not yet tried a Goddess Fish **Facebook party**, and the company I used several years ago seems to be no lon-ger active. However, do-it-yourself Facebook parties are explained by author K.R. Thompson on *The Maze*: http://kimiversonheadlee.blogspot.com/2015/09/the-busi-ness-of-writing-diy-facebook.html.

4A5. In-Person Events

As an independent author I sell more print copies in person than via online catalogs, so I make every effort to attend as many of these as my schedule and budget and family's patience allow. If you wish to be placed on the guest list at conventions—many of which come with perks such as free membership and table space for signing and selling books—contact the organizing committee at least six months in advance. If you can provide additional content, such as participating in panels or presenting a workshop, all the better.

4A6. Print Media

This aspect doesn't get as much attention in the promotion plan as it used to, but it's still a good idea to keep your local news media outlets in mind. Prepare a page-turner of a press release, keep it short and snappy but make sure to include all your contact information, and submit it to their news desk at least two weeks in advance.

4A7. Audio/Visual Media (Podcasts, Radio, TV)

One of my longtime writer-friends produces a weekly podcast about his books. That's not my thing, but if it happens to be yours, by all means go for it. I have been interviewed during conventions for podcasts, which is a lot of fun. If your budget is big enough to pay for radio and TV advertising, all the more power to you. A potentially less expensive means to obtain radio advertising is to donate a "day sponsorship" to your local National Public Radio member station, which entitles the advertiser to five announcements broadcast throughout the day in question. In addition, the sponsorship is at least partially tax deductible. The NPR sponsorship link (http://www.npr.org/about-npr/187533209/major-gifts) does not talk about day sponsorships, but it provides an email address for inquiries.

4A8. Book Trailers

YOU CAN produce these yourself or you can invest in high-quality products that look like you're watching a movie trailer. My YouTube channel (http://www.youtube.com/user/gyanhumara) features specimens at both ends of the production spectrum. The person who created my most impressive trailers is no longer in the business, but Videos by O (http://videosbyo.blogspot.com/) does a great job on several types of projects and allows the client to choose the payment that fits his or her budget.

Great information about do-it-yourself book trailers may be viewed on *The Maze*, reblogged with permission of author Nancy Cohen:

- PART 1. "Do Your Homework!" (http://kimiversonheadlee.blogspot.com/2015/09/the-business-of-writing-do-your.html)
- PART 2. "Now What?" (http://kimiversonheadlee.blogspot.com/2015/09/the-business-of-writing-now-what-diy.html)

4A9. Promotional Materials

THESE ITEMS come in all shapes, sizes, and functions: bookmarks, note cards, charms and other book-related jewelry, display banners, tote bags, decks of playing cards, nail files, pens, matchboxes, candy bar wrappers, and a jillion other items collectively classified as swag. But their primary purpose should be to sell your book. The most efficient way to accomplish this is to incorporate your book's QR code (that little square box with the odd bar code that smartphones with a QR code reader app can interpret) into whatever you design. Refer to that section later in this chapter for further information.

4A10. Overview of Promotional Opportunities

FREE AND paid book-promotion sites, discussed later in this chapter, are a must in your promotion plan, though you do need to follow each site's rules for your book's genre, content, length, number of reviews, star rating, promotional price, and lead time for your preferred promotion date.

Most free-promo sites offer paid options to guarantee advertising in their newsletters or on their websites.

If you run a blog, you can set up exchange agreements with your author-friends to spotlight each other's books now and then, which is another excellent source of exposure that typically costs no more than an hour of your time to arrange and compose. Having your media kit handy will cut down on that time investment.

4A11. Blogging Overview

WHEN I first took the plunge to actively expand my social network, everyone said I needed to start a blog. So I did. And it got very few views, something on the order of maybe a couple of dozen a day. To be honest, that was a couple of dozen more than I was expecting, since I had (foolishly, I admit) neglected the "care and feeding" of my readership and could host my entire fan base in my living room.

To increase blog reach, I took the following steps:

- I joined Facebook and, eventually, Twitter and now share blog posts to those platforms on a regular basis.
- I set up automatic cross-posting of my blog to my author profiles on About.me, Goodreads, and Amazon, and posts get automatically shared to my Google+ profile by Blogger.
- I started scheduling promo posts for other authors in exchange for their posting of my book spotlights on their blogs.
- I engaged the services of auto-tweeting and auto-retweeting apps, both of which have long since been suspended by Twitter, but these were instrumental in boosting my following up over the five thousand mark. Now I'm pushing twenty thousand and growing daily, thanks to judicious tweeting and retweeting with Hootsuite (http://hootsuite.com/).
- I started scheduling virtual book tours, which have spread the word even farther into the blogosphere. Whenever possible, I visit the promo pages and

thank the bloggers for hosting and reviewing my books, and I answer other visitors' questions too.
- I began posting a version of my monthly newsletter, *The Dawnflier* (http://eepurl.com/boiQ0z).
- I set up Rafflecopter (https://www.rafflecopter.com/pricing) contests in conjunction with my blog tours, and I run a monthly contest via Amazon to which *The Dawnflier* subscribers get first crack.
- I joined Triberr (http://triberr.com/), a post-sharing service for bloggers of which the free service is just fine for my needs, and I became a member of more than fifty tribes there. Now my potential Twitter reach is over twenty-one million thanks to the sharing of posts by my thousand-plus tribemates. This has been the single biggest factor in jumping my blog's page views.

Other potentially useful post-sharing software that I haven't evaluated yet includes Roundteam (https://roundteam.co/), Tweet Jukebox (http://www.tweetjukebox.com/), and Feed140 (https://feed140.net/home). I confess that I'm hesitant to try them because Hootsuite is joined at Twitter's hip and has proven to be a stable platform, and I've invested on the order of a month's worth of work in establishing my vast collection of tweets that I reuse.

There are other social media platforms I haven't mentioned, mainly because I don't keep a presence on them or I use them strictly for professional rather than promotional reasons (e.g., LinkedIn; https://www.linkedin.com/in/kimheadlee). I do recommend that you claim your name on those platforms, however, in case you change your mind and decide to participate at a future date.

4A12. Promotional Content

WHETHER IT'S a blog, a Pinterest board, or profiles on Facebook or Twitter or some other platform, when I visit another author's page, I am turned off when the content is exclusively about his or her own books. Think about it, people: it's like tuning to a shopping channel. At least, that's how I imagine it would be like if I ever did tune to a shopping channel.

Posting news about your books is essential for spreading the word, but balancing that content with other items will keep your readers coming back for more. Ancillary content should be driven by your personality and likes. I achieve balance by:

- SCHEDULING spotlights of my friends' books on my blog
- PARTICIPATING as a book tour host for other authors
- CROSS-POSTING my Pinterest pins to my Twitter account and, on occasion, to my personal Facebook profile or author page
- SHARING an excerpt each week—along with a writing tip or a nonwriting introduction—from my current work in progress
- POSTING my latest *Business of Writing* topics
- OCCASIONALLY posting an article on my blog about a nonwriting or nonbook topic that interests me, such as this post about my having met in person one of the last living Pearl Harbor survivors (http://kimiversonheadlee.blogspot.com/2014/11/veterans-day-

2014-with-herb-weatherwax.html)

- USING my Facebook personal profile to interact with my family and friends—here I post fun slice-of-life snippets, humor, and links to nonwriting articles I enjoy
- AUTOMATICALLY cross-posting my Facebook posts to Twitter (if I want the Facebook post to look as if it originated on Twitter, I keep it less than 140 characters and don't include a link)
- USING my Facebook author and fan pages to post research-related articles as well as updates about my books
- SHARING other authors' Facebook posts about their books
- VISITING the Twitter profile of each person who follows me

I will perhaps retweet a thing or three, and I follow back as many accounts as possible within the bounds of my conscience. If you discover that I have blocked your account, it means that I found your content objectionable. Among the accounts that I don't block but don't follow back are those that advertise selling followers, those whose content is mildly objectionable or is not provided in English, and those wherein the profile and/or cover pics appear stalker-y.

By the way, if you're one of those authors out on an ego trip to amass what appears to be a huge fan base by following me and then unfollowing within a nanosecond of my following you, be aware that I check my Crowdfire (http://crowdfireapp.com/) numbers daily and will unfollow you. I respectfully advise that you reevaluate the practice and obtain your ego stroking from your book sales and reviews.

- SCHEDULING my book-related tweets no more frequently than once an hour—if you ever happen to see more frequency than that from me, it's because I'm doing a onetime tweet of a blog tour page or something along those lines
- SCHEDULING the sharing of other bloggers' posts that appear in my Triberr stream every day

Good advice for establishing balanced content is to follow the rule of thirds: one-third of your content posted in support of others, one-third about your nonwriting interests, and one-third about your books. I don't recall where I saw this rule mentioned, but I do like the concept and try to follow it myself whenever possible.

4B. The Author Blog, or "How Not to Annoy Your Visitors"

WHEN I became a published novelist with the sale of my manuscript *Dawnflight* to Simon & Schuster in 1997, the Internet was taking its first baby steps, long before social media in general, and blogging specifically, was a gleam in anybody's eye. When blogging started to become popular, my writing career was in hiatus.

"Why bother blogging?" I asked myself. Lacking a sufficient answer, I did not begin a blog in those days.

Kayelle Allen, founder of Marketing for Romance Writers, offers a great take on that question:

> A blog is a way of having fresh content on your website every day. How often can you release a new book? Probably not often enough to get people to come back to your website on a regular basis. Blogging brings people, and can generate followers for your blog, and for your social media.

> **Ask yourself—so what?**

> Why does that matter? Because those people who come back are people who have heard of you. When people buy books, they buy books that interest them, and they buy books by authors they know. They've learned that the

author will give them a good read. Name recognition in this business is a major key to success. Read the rest of her excellent article here (http://mfrw.blogspot.com/2015/10/why-blog.html).

In mathematical terms, the average fiction reader will not take a chance on a novel until she or he has heard mention of the author or book at least seven times. An author blog is an excellent way to help improve those odds... providing the author follows some basic advice about blog structure and content.

4B1. Blog Structure

BLOG STRUCTURE includes the platform, layout, and elements included with each page or post.

Blogging platform

IF YOU haven't yet established a blog, the first decision you'll face is which blogging platform to use. The two major players are Blogger and WordPress.

I picked Blogger in 2013 because it's free and easy, with *free* being the more important consideration since I have been an HTML coder for decades and already had a static website. Where Blogger makes things easy for me is in the blog post publishing process, since my static site required use of file transfer protocol software to perform uploads whenever I wanted to tweak a page. This functionality is built in to Blogger (and, I later learned, WordPress), so that's one less tool I have to worry about.

Then I started hearing about WordPress and how those sites look more professional. For a while, I considered running both a Blogger and a WordPress blog, but I have since abandoned that plan.

Why?

Mainly because I get the distinct impression that the free version of WordPress will not support my needs as an author-blogger. One of the best (and also free) blog-marketing tools I've discovered is Triberr, and I often hear bloggers grumble about how difficult it is to get their WordPress blogs set up to feed the Triberr stream. And even when those bloggers do get their WordPress posts to show up in the feed, there are issues about the display of images and content.

I have neither the time nor patience to wrestle with technological issues like that, and I am not interested in paying WordPress to solve those issues for me when Blogger already does what I need for free.

Blog layout

THERE ARE nigh as many ways to lay out a blog as there are bloggers on the planet. Because my list of published full-length novels is only six at present, I have elected to devote one static blog page to each, plus a page for my personal appearances.

If you have five or more books in print and want to set up static pages, you might choose to organize your books by series or genre to maintain a manageable page count.

The whole point to a blog's layout is to present pertinent information without overwhelming the visitor.

At first I had embedded my book trailers' YouTube code in *The Maze*'s sidebar, and I repeated that code on the books' dedicated pages. I have since replaced the sidebar trailer embeds with the book covers. Although all my trailers are well worth watching and are especially impressive on big-screen TVs, since they are very similar to movie trailers, it's the cover that is an author's first and best chance of engaging a potential reader.

I also rearranged the order and elected to place my social media info and newsletter signup at the top of the sidebar, above my books. One of the things that turns me off when I visit an author's blog is to be inundated with book covers and buy links right from the start, so I've tried not to do that to *The Maze*'s visitors.

Originally I had developed a dedicated page for listing my giveaways, but I found that it's easier to mention them on individual blog posts rather than to keep updating the giveaway page. I still have that page saved as a draft in case I ever decide to rearrange *The Maze* again.

Blog elements

INDIVIDUAL BLOG elements are legion, but the basic necessities for an author blog include the display of book covers, buy links, and social media following opportunities.

I've already chimed in on the subject of book cover placement—again, the key is to disseminate the information without turning off the reader. Having the social media following opportunities placed in a prominent position is important too, because they are going to be more chances for you and your books to reach that magic seven-mentions threshold for clinching the sale.

Displaying graphic elements for the various social media sites is a fine practice, but please do not code them to reappear on the screen like a cloud of hopeful puppies as the visitor pages down the post. I find that annoying, and I will leave your blog faster than you can blink, never to return.

Another turnoff for me is to be hit with a "sign up for

this blog" popup immediately upon visiting the site. Even with blogs I visit on a regular basis, I never subscribe to them—I'm drowning in emails as it is—so to be bombarded with a request when all I want to do is read one post is annoying.

In case you haven't figured it out, annoyed blog visitors will never buy your book.

4B2. Blog Content

THE AMUSING *Lili's Travel Plans* blog has some great advice regarding all those posts you see in your Twitter feed that start with "How To" or "*X* Tips for Doing *Y,*" if you're tempted to structure your posts in either of those ways. Unless you want to appear spammer-y, try to avoid those tactics in your headlines. Read the full take on why here: http://www.lilistravelplans.com/8-tips-for-getting-tons-of-traffic-to-your-blog-and-making-lots-of-money-with-it-and-why-im-not-following-them/.

A Triberr tribemate of mine, a blogging team known as "e-Books India," could have called one of their posts "5 Tips for Becoming a Better Author-Blogger" but instead titled it "How Authors Can Become Better Bloggers" (http://e-booksindia.com/how-authors-can-become-better-bloggers/).

That article rightly advises author-bloggers to concentrate on developing a focus for the blog, being mindful of content, promoting your book with blog tours where you contribute guest posts to other blogs, building community by responding to comments in an engaging yet professional way, and creating a regular blogging schedule. To that impressive list I add the suggestion to support other authors by participating as a blog-tour host.

The creation of positive karma is always a good thing for everyone involved.

Author Nikki Woods drills down even further to offer the following list of specific must-haves for content on an author's blog:

1. Excerpts from your works in progress
2. Writing tips
3. Personal anecdotes
4. Insight into your writing process
5. Inspiration for your writing

Her complete article may be viewed here: http://www.nikkiwoodsmedia.com/5-author-blog/. I concur with her list, and I do offer these items from time to time on *The Maze*. Often, I combine items in a single post, such as a personal anecdote or aspect of inspiration with a work-in-progress excerpt.

What you elect to share with the world will be in direct relation to your comfort level.

If by now you're feeling a bit overwhelmed, please don't be.

The key to all of this is to achieve a balance of content so that your blog reflects whatever brand you have established as an author but does not appear as a 24/7 infomercial about your books. Programming that sort of content in the sidebar, as I have done on *The Maze*, is akin to TV channels pasting their logos into the corner of your screen: it's there if the visitor chooses to see it, but it can be tuned out while she or he is viewing the featured post.

4C. Search Engine Optimization for Author-Bloggers, or "Say... What?"

Say-oh sayoh say say-oh sayoh say say-oh sayoh say sayoh say-oh...

WHAT? YOU MEAN those aren't the introductory lyrics to "Pompeii" by Bastille?

But I'll bet I got your attention with the earworm.

By "say-oh" I mean SEO, search engine optimization, which may seem like just as much gibberish as "say-oh" does.

I hope to change that for you.

Kayelle Allen of MFRW has written a brilliant article about SEO and how you can harness its power. Her definitions are especially insightful:

SEO: Search Engine Optimization—the process by which we gear our websites to be searchable by search engines such as Google, Bing, Yahoo, and others.

Keyword: A significant word used in indexing or cataloging, or in labeling other text. For example, some genre keywords are romance, historical, fantasy, scifi, highlander, etc.

Label: These are similar to keywords, but are brief descriptions given for purposes of identification.

Hashtag: a word embedded in a searchable text on sites such as Twitter, Facebook, and other social media. These words (or tags) are preceded by the symbol # which is also called a hashmark, hence the term, "hashtag."
Read her full article about SEO here: http://mfrw.blogspot.com/2015/12/how-to-use-seo.html.

I don't always follow all the steps that she recommends for upping the SEO ante for my posts, but I usually can check off having a central theme, the length requirement (at least 300 words), putting a keyword or hashtag in the post's title, and applying appropriate labels.

The biggest key to optimizing the searchability of your content, whatever type of blog you run, is to generate a strong combination of keywords, labels, and hashtags so that search engines stand a better chance of finding your posts.

Another good article about writing SEO-friendly blog posts was written by Julie Petersen on the *IFTISEO* blog (http://www.iftiseo.com/2015/12/7-tips-to-write-seo-friendly-blog-posts.html). The primary takeaway from her article is the linking to related posts. This technique is an easy way to increase the relevance of both posts in SEO algorithms.

If you've gone to the geek side, you can play with this keyword density checker tool: http://smallseotools.com/keyword-density-checker/ thanks to a comment in Julie Petersen's post. This tool checks everything, including strings of numbers, but it makes for an interesting exercise if you're into statistics.

Taylor Manning on the *Mad Lemmings* blog explains SEO optimization for images here: http://madlemmings.com/2016/01/11/seo-image-optimization/.

While much of Taylor Manning's advice is geared toward HTML programmers at an advanced level, there are some tricks the average blogger can employ, such as naming one's images to reflect keywords relevant to the post in which the image is used.

I have taken this advice to rename book covers that I send to other bloggers for upload; for example, "Dawnflight-Kim-Headlee-Arthurian-legends.jpg." To avail yourself of this SEO feature, you must use hyphens rather than spaces or underscore characters.

"Where do we begin?
The rubble or our sins?"*

Begin with creating a clear message that's laden with keywords. I cannot absolve anyone's SEO sins, but I do know that if you apply solid optimization techniques, the rubble will take care of itself.

*EXCERPTED from "Pompeii," written by Dan Smith and performed by Bastille, Virgin Records, 2013.

4D. Waxing Technical, Part 1: Introduction to Amazon's Kindle Book Previewer

IF YOU THOUGHT the SEO section was technical, just wait till you dive into this one. No worries; Lifeguard Kim will do her best to keep you afloat amid the jargon.

I have been a programmer since the days when to program a computer meant flipping a series of switches on its console… and a deck of punched cards was a vast improvement. So please forgive me if I geek out on you a bit here. I promise I will make it up to you later.

Early in 2016 the wit-heads behind the arrow-smile at Amazon rolled out a feature that I like: the embeddable Kindle book previewer.

Why is the Kindle book previewer useful to author-bloggers?

I can think of several reasons:

- THE cover images are stored on Amazon's servers, not yours. This can be a critical asset if you are running short on room on your blog's server.
- THE covers load faster for blog visitors, an important way to increase the chances of them clicking through on your book's buy link.
- THE latest cover image is always displayed, again saving you the trouble and storage requirements of uploading new covers to your blog.
- AMAZON gives you access to "Preview," "Buy," and

"Share" options without a visitor ever having to leave your page. For those of us with multiple titles, this is a fantastic way to keep readers engaged with our blog's content. The longer the engagement, the better the chances of landing the sale.

Implementing the Kindle book previewer is as easy as one-two-three, as shown in Amazon's tutorial on this page: http://www.amazon.com/b?ie=UT-F8&node=13489836011. The process allows you to generate either a link or a chunk of HTML code.

In case you're too busy to type in the link, the basic steps are:

1. DISPLAY the Amazon product page of the Kindle book for which you want to generate the preview link or code.

   Note 1: If you are an Amazon affiliate, do not display the page with your affiliate tag; Amazon's browser software doesn't know how to process that, and the page will sit and spin forever. Not to worry, however; they give you an opportunity to specify your affiliate ID in the code-generation popup window.

   Note 2: The most compact form of the Amazon product link for your book, without having to grind it through link-shortening software, is http://www.amazon.com/dp/**Your Books ASIN** where ASIN is the ten-digit identification Amazon has assigned to your book. For example, the Amazon e-book link for my novel *Dawnflight* is: http://www.amazon.com/dp/B00BLNN6XS

2. On the product page, click the <Embed> link. It is located in the same line with all the other sharing options (email, Facebook, etc.) underneath the long bar that reads "Add to List."

Note 3: If you are working off a tablet or an even smaller screen, you will have to scroll down a bit to find the <Embed> hyperlink.

3. On the popup window, select either the "Get a link (URL)" (the default) or "Embed on your site (HTML)" option, and then copy the result by clicking in the display area and pressing the <CTRL> (or <COMMAND> on Mac devices) and <C> keys. (To dump the contents of the paste buffer into another application, press <CTRL><V> or <COMMAND><V>.) These are near-universal hot key shortcuts that have been staples of computer operating systems since the introduction of keyboards as input devices.

Note 4: If you have an Amazon affiliate ID, click the link to enter your ID before you copy the code or link. Type your ID where they tell you to and the system will update the result as you watch. Then click in the box displaying the code or link, and copy it.

If you have requested a link, you will see something like this:

https://read.amazon.com/kp/embed?asin=**Your_Books_ASIN**&preview=newtab&linkCode=k-pe&ref_=cm_sw_r_kb_dp_5G2hxb127N-HFS&tag=**Your_Amazon_Affiliate_ID**

To save yourself the hassle of these three steps, create a copy of the above link and replace "**Your_Books_ASIN**" and "**Your_Amazon_Affiliate_ID**," or delete all text beginning with "&tag" to the end of the string if you don't have an affiliate ID, and you're all set to embed the link.

The link code gets pasted between the "" in your <A HREF=""> HTML tag.

If you have requested an HTML fragment, you'll get:

<iframe type="text/html" width="336" height="550" frameborder="0" allowfullscreen style="max-width:100%" src="https://read. amazon.com/kp/card?asin=**Your_Books_ ASIN**&preview=inline&linkCode=kpe&ref_=cm_ sw_r_kb_dp_5G2hxb127NHFS&tag=Your_Amazon_ Affiliate_ID" ></iframe>

Same drill as with the link as far as customizing this fragment for your needs, but do not delete the "></ iframe>" part at the end of the fragment.

On my blog I go into detail about how to customize the HTML to "float" the book's cover with text flowing to one side or the other, as well as reducing the cover's size as in my blog's sidebar images. Since the post is far more technical than this introduction is, with lots of HTML examples that are easier to copy and paste from the blog rather than this book, I commend to your attention this link: http://kimiversonheadlee.blogspot.com/2016/05/ the-business-of-writing-advanced.html.

4E. Hit 'Em with Your Best Shot: The Author Newsletter

YEARS AGO, WHEN I used to receive professionally printed authors' newsletters in the mail, I didn't adopt the tactic because I would have had trouble coming up with something new to report every month.

This was at the close of the millennium when traditional publishing was the norm, with a few small presses struggling to keep their doors open for love of the written word rather than the bottom line. As a traditional-published author, I was tied to my publisher's schedule and whims regarding whether they would reprint my novels or acquire their sequels, issue them in a different format, or exploit ancillary rights such as audiobook and foreign translations.

Sure, I could have reported news of book signings, lectures, and other personal appearances, but without the Really Big News to announce of another imminent release, I didn't see the point of wasting all that postage.

With the advent of social media as an inexpensive tool for self-promotion, of course, all of that has changed.

Beverly Bateman raises the question of "Do I or don't I?" publish an author newsletter on *Blogging With Beverly*: http://beverleybateman.blogspot.com/2015/10/do-i-or-dont-i.html.

Her post was inspired by a podcast she had listened to for increasing email subscribers. The podcaster suggested the publication of weekly newsletters. I cannot envision myself ever sending weekly newsletters—not due to lack of content, because I have a lot more news to report these days with regard to the progress of audiobooks, graphic novels, and new releases—but because I'd never get any new writing done.

Tip #10 of BookBub's "98 Book Marketing Tips" (http://insights.bookbub.com/book-marketing-ideas/) applies to the topic of the author newsletter:

> **10. Welcome new subscribers with an email autoresponse.** When people subscribe to updates from you via your website, send them a welcome email including either a link to a permafree ebook, sample chapters, or some sort of freebie as a "thank you" for signing up.

I offer my permafree title, *The Color of Vengeance*, to new subscribers. If you don't have a free book, you could offer a sample chapter of your latest work in progress, an Amazon giveaway link, or something else along those lines.

I have established a first-of-the-month publication schedule for my newsletter, *The Dawnflier* (http://eepurl.com/boiQ0z), and I am pleased with how it's working out.

If you still need convincing, or if you're convinced you want to start a newsletter but aren't sure where to begin, this article by Penny Sansevieri, CEO and founder of Author Marketing Experts, contains many excellent points about content and other considerations: http://www.amarketingexpert.com/how-your-newsletter-can-get-you-more-readers-visibility-and-sales/.

One thing the article does not address is the email

delivery service. My original email server would lock me out if it noticed me sending huge batches of emails. That server is hosted by GoDaddy (http://www.godaddy.com), but I've heard of this happening to Gmail accounts too.

That's why I have started a list hosted by MailChimp (http://www.mailchimp.com). If I ever get enough subscribers to necessitate paying for the professional level of service, that will be a great day! But for now the free version does everything I need. There's a bit of a learning curve to figure out "campaign" (i.e., newsletter) design, but once I got over that hump and discovered the "save as template" option, subsequent newsletter designs have been a snap.

Whether you do or don't publish a periodic email newsletter is entirely up to you, of course, but I've found that it's an excellent way to connect with my readers.

4F. Hit 'Em Again: Email Marketing for Books

THE PUBLICIST I hired to help promote my second NY-published novel, *Liberty*, had a saying that went something like this:

> Marketing requires three elements:
> skill, money, and time.
> What you lack in one element,
> you must make up for by applying the other two.

She is no longer in the PR business, but her words continue to guide me, and I hope they resonate with you too.

If you lack the money to hire personnel to market your book, you cannot just ignore the promoting and hope for the best. That's how I found myself having to rebuild my audience from scratch in 2013 when I decided to dive into the shark tank that is independent publishing.

Trust me on this point: you need to pour your own time into self-promotion and become adept at using the requisite software tools.

The most obvious form of free email marketing is for you to distribute your own newsletter, as I discussed in the previous section. Read on for even more email-marketing options, free as well as paid.

4F1. Free Email Marketing Other Than Your Own Newsletter

IT IS possible to market your book online for free.

That said, many sites have either excruciatingly long (on the order of six months) queues for their free email promo opportunities, have converted to paid advertising only, or have disappeared altogether. Since the list for free email book promotions is an ever-changing one, I invite you to run an Internet search of that phrase.

Some that don't appear to be going anywhere for the time being include:

- AWESOME Gang (http://awesomegang.com/submit-your-book/)
- BOOKS on the Knob (https://docs.google.com/forms/d/1DlL2gaFaDtcTbjZ-STE-zsGD4HOvHRccShMyycCgqfGs/viewform)
- BOOKWORMS and Writers (http://www.bookwormsandwriters.com/)
- BOOKZIO (http://www.bookzio.com/submit-a-listing/)
- DISCOUNT Book Man (http://discountbookman.com/book-promotion/)
- EBOOKASAURUS (http://ebookasaurus.com/free-book-listing/)
- EBOOKS Habit (http://ebookshabit.com/for-authors/)
- EREADER Girl (http://ereadergirl.com/submit-your-ebook/)
- EVERY Writer Resource (http://everywritersre-

source.com/selfpublished/submit-your-book/)
- FREE Book Dude (http://www.freebookdude.com/2016/05/advertising-and-promotion-options-with.html)
- FREE99BOOKS (http://free99books.com/author/add)
- FRUGAL Freebies (http://www.frugal-freebies.com/p/submit-freebie.html)
- GREAT Books Great Deals (https://greatbooksgreat-deals.wufoo.com/forms/gbgd-authors/)
- INDIE Book of the Day (http://indiebookoftheday.com/authors/free-on-kindle-listing/)
- IT'S Write Now (http://itswritenow.com/submit-your-book/)
- KINDLE Book Promos (http://kindlebookpromos.luckycinda.com/?page_id=283)
- PEOPLE Reads (http://www.peoplereads.com/list-your-ebook)
- READING Deals (http://readingdeals.com/submit-ebook)
- *ROMANCE Lives Forever* blog (http://romancelivesforever.blogspot.com/p/guest-blogger-faqs.html)
- ROMANCE Readers Club (http://romancereadersclub.com/for-authors/)
- ROMANCE Rock Stars (http://romancerockstars.com/index.php/author-services/)
- THE eReader Cafe (http://theereadercafe.com/promote-your-books/)

You need to read all the fine print at each site prior to submitting your title for consideration. Some sites allow for resubmission of books, or the submission of an additional book in your backlist after a set number of days or months, and some have restrictions on your book's pricing or how often an author may promote one or more titles.

Another option—not free, but it entails a onetime cost, so it should pay for itself sooner rather than later—is to purchase the Kindle Direct Return on Investment browser plugin offered by 5MinutePublishing. The direct link to the software is (http://www.5minutepublishing.com/dashboard/kdroi/), though the site may require you to first sign up for their newsletter, and I do apologize for that annoyance.

I've found KDROI to be well worth any momentary annoyance, however, since it allows me to schedule free, permafree, and $0.99 promos with approximately two dozen sites at a time.

I'm starting to see advertisements for similar services offered by other companies, and I will update this section after I have investigated them.

4F2. Paid Email Marketing Other Than BookBub

BOOKBUB (http://www.bookbub.com/partners) is so far the only paid advertising venue I've discovered wherein the royalties earned from resulting downloads have exceeded the cost of the promotion. It's a notoriously tough nut to crack, however, so it gets its own section in this book.

For all paid advertising except BookBub, you should approach the promotion with the primary goal of raising awareness of your book. Most sites with a sizable mailing list should give you a modest bump in sales, but recall that seven-mentions threshold, and don't be discouraged if you don't break even on these lesser promotion venues.

Since April 2015, I have been experimenting with paid advertising—Twitter, Facebook, and website promos in addition to email lists—for most of my books, even my permafree and limited-free offerings. My general findings to date:

- TWITTER-ONLY packages are not worth it. Period. It's like dropping leaflets about your book from one hundred thousand feet above the planet and hoping they will land where readers will find them and act upon them. In reality, most of the leaflets will land in the ocean. And we all know what sorts of readers fish are.
- SAME with Facebook-only and website-only packages. Maybe not quite as bad as broadcasting to the Twitterverse, but close. These two options do carry the advantage of having a bit more permanence than Twitter, where your tweets get flushed off users' screens within mere nanoseconds. Though the feed-flushing happens with Facebook too, you do have the option of curating posts to preserve them on your author page. (Not to be outdone, Twitter now offers tweet curation called "moments," but I've been too busy finishing this book to experiment with that option. The "pinned tweet" function works just fine for my campaign needs.)

This left paid email advertising, and for the six months of my experiment (April–October 2015), I was beginning to believe those weren't worth it either.

In those days, I had yet to realize that marketing is not about landing sales.

An Internet search will yield a bunch of paid email

services, but the ones I've had the best experiences with are:

- **Book Barbarian** (http://bookbarbarian.com/ad-requirements/). Science Fiction and Fantasy genres only; this includes paranormal romance, fantasy romance, and so forth. It's primarily an email advertising service, but pricing includes a permanent link on their website and promotions on Facebook, Google+, and Twitter. Their email subscriber list numbers only in the low thousands, but they are dedicated science fiction and fantasy readers, so the click-through rate is much higher. They will waive their "first book of a series only" rule if you want to pay extra to promote the first two books, but in general I have found that paying to promote subsequent books in a series is not worth it. Your best advertising is always the first book.

- **Books Butterfly.** Paid advertising for permafree (http://www.booksbutterfly.com/bookpromotion/permafreebookpromotion/), limited free (http://www.booksbutterfly.com/bookpromotion/freebookpromotion/), $0.99 (http://www.booksbutterfly.com/bookpromotion/paidbookpromotion/), box sets (http://www.booksbutterfly.com/bookpromotion/boxsetpromotion/), and single books priced at more than $1.00 (http://www.booksbutterfly.com/bookpromotion/paidebookpromotion/). Pricing is based upon "guaranteed" download numbers, which I agree seems a bit iffy, but my books haven't experienced an issue with that. A new wrinkle is they no longer offer a prorated refund if your Books Butterfly promo runs in conjunction with BookBub. However, this is a great option to use in combination with BookBub to keep your book's momentum going.

- **eBook Soda** (http://www.ebooksoda.com/authors/). Flat fee regardless of genre or sale price, making it a good value, especially when used in conjunction with other promotions. Limitations: minimum length restrictions and your book must be rated at least 3.5 with eight or more reviews unless the book is a new release.

- **eReader News Today** (http://ereadernewstoday.com/pricing/). This site used to be the be-all, end-all of e-book marketing until BookBub dethroned it, but it still packs a wallop if you can get your book selected for promotion; as with BookBub, submissions are juried. Cost varies by genre and the book's promotional pricing. Main restrictions are that the book must be at least 125 pages, listed on Amazon, and not promoted on ENT in the past ninety days.

- **Genre Pulse** (http://www.genrepulse.com/how-it-works/). Your book must be $0.99 or free. They offer full mailing list and genre-specific mailing list promo options, and they give coupons to repeat advertisers that are good for the full promo option. The biggest thing I like about Genre Pulse is the campaign link they give you, which allows you to see your click-through statistics. I do geek out on the statistics, in case you haven't already figured this out.

- **The Fussy Librarian** (http://www.thefussylibrarian.com/for-authors/). Another site where the cost varies by genre, but they don't charge you more if your promotional price is higher than $0.99. They encourage you to add on genres at half off the regular advertising rate, but I've found that to be not worth it even with any discount coupon I might have received. Your book must have at least ten reviews on Amazon with an average 4.0 rating, unless it's a new release and you have at least one other book in your backlist that has the minimum ten reviews and 4.0 rating. The book you're advertising must be priced at $5.99 or less, and there are no length restrictions.

Paid email services I may try again at some point:

- **BETTY BookFreak** (http://bettybookfreak.com/authors/). This used to be a free site; they now charge a modest but variable fee for placement depending on what type of listing you want (Daily Pick, New Release, or Daily Underdog), rather than by genre. They also have an interesting option I have not seen with any other paid email service: $30.00 will get you placement on their welcome newsletter to new subscribers for thirty days. You may capitalize on this if your book is free and if you are willing to commit your title to that long of a promotion period.

- **BOOKGORILLA** (http://www.bookgorilla.com/advertise). As of this writing, it still costs only $50.00 to feature one $0.99 book, regardless of its length or genre, which is not bad for an email list that boasts more than three hundred fifty thousand subscribers. Starred title promotion (first page of their daily email) is a $100.00 add-on charge, and that's not worth it unless you are promoting a *New York Times* or *USA Today* best-seller (87 percent subscriber reach) or your book falls into one of the most popular genres among subscribers (mysteries enjoy a 55 percent subscriber reach; most romance subgenres fall in the mid-30-percent range). A distinct drawback is that their lead time for scheduling promotions is too far out (a minimum of six weeks) to coordinate with a BookBub deal.

- **BOOKSENDS** (http://booksends.com/advertise.php). They charge different rates by genre and book's price. Unless you enjoy flushing your money down the stink hole, do not pay them extra for the privilege of putting your Amazon affiliate tag on a free book, since that gains you nothing. I also advise not paying the extra fee for Facebook or EReaderIQ promotion either.

- **READ Cheaply** (http://readcheaply.com/partners/). I used this service when it was free. Now they charge $25.00 and up for promoting full-length books, and genre subscriber list sizes range from fifteen to sixty-five thousand.

Paid services I've heard good reports about but haven't yet tried:

- **DIGITAL Book Today** (http://digitalbooktoday.com/join-our-team/paid-and-free-promotions/). This site has several free as well as paid promotion options, including website advertisements. Their email subscriber list stands at about sixteen thousand readers.

- **EYE on Romance** (http://www.eyeonromance.com/forauthors.cfm). This website hit me with four pop-ups (three of them were unique, and one repeated after I closed it the first time) within the first thirty seconds of my visit, and the pricing for various services was far higher than I expected. But if you are trying to market your romance novels and can get past the sticker shock and site annoyances, advertising with them may be an option for you.

- **THE Romance Reviews** (http://www.theromancer-eviews.com/advertise.php). Predominant focus is on website, Twitter, and Facebook advertising, with more than thirty thousand followers on each social media platform, but as of this writing they advertise an email subscriber list of 16,500 romance readers.

4F3. The Roller Coaster of Paid Email Book Marketing: BookBub

IF YOUR book meets the minimum length requirements and is great enough to pass the ENT jurying process, then chances are better than good that you can score a BookBub promotion too.

There are very few pleasures I enjoy in life more than roller coasters: the excruciating wait of the queue; the niggling anxiety of climbing into the car; the mounting anticipation as the train grinds up that first and steepest incline; the moment of, "Oh, crap, what have I gotten myself into?!?" at the pinnacle; the jaw-dropping, gut-wrenching burst of speed; the sheer joy of feeling the wind through my hair and fingers as I let go of the rail and squeal my vocal cords raw!

The final coast back into the station brings a blessed sense of relief... coupled with the intense urge to race back into the queue to do it all over again.

Although a near-fatal car wreck in 2003 has left me with permanent pins in my neck and has thrown the brakes on my amusement-park adventures, I can relive the sensation through BookBub feature promotions of my novels.

The queue

OF ALL the paid promotional sites that I've tried for my books (sizes of mailing lists aside), BookBub is unique for its rule that a book not be offered at your specified promotional price for more than fourteen days out of the past ninety. The reason is tied to the way Amazon calculates royalties based on your book's average price for the past thirty days.

BookBub has some way of checking your past Amazon pricing, as I discovered when I tried submitting my first featured deal. It was rejected on the grounds that I had violated the fourteen-day pricing rule at a time when I was trying to build my readership by offering all my titles at $0.99 or free for months at a stretch.

Since I wasn't sure which book I would be able to place with BookBub first, I gritted my teeth and raised prices on all my full-length novels. This meant suffering next to nothing in sales during that excruciating period, but—as with the roller-coaster queue—the torture eased once BookBub informed me of *Dawnflight*'s selection on 2/8/2016.

The end of the queue had lurched into sight at last!

Climbing into the car

SOMETIMES WITH coasters you have a choice of cars to ride in, and sometimes you don't. Give me a choice and I will sit in the front seat of the first car every time.

Although you can specify a preferred promotional period, every article I've read about landing a BookBub promotion advises that your chances of being selected improve markedly if you tell them your dates are flexible, and that's what I did.

I chose to follow Amazon's KDP Select pricing model

and have my $0.99 deal run five days, though for BookBub I specified that the deal would end a day sooner. BookBub gives dire warnings about ending your deal prematurely, and I wanted to make sure that I wouldn't get banned from the ride forever on my very first trip down the rails.

At this point the roller-coaster analogy doesn't match a BookBub promo, for the stage of grinding up the first and steepest incline is switched with:

"Oh, crap, what have I gotten myself into?!?"

I PAID $380.00 for a US-only feature in the fantasy category, for which BookBub at that time (February 2016) reported a subscriber list of more than 1,400,000. Five months later, when I booked my $0.99 deal in the same category for *King Arthur's Sister in Washington's Court*, the cost for a US-only feature had increased to $400.00 to reach 1,600,000 subscribers.

If a year earlier you had told me that I would have been *excited* to shell out that much money for one email promotional advertisement for one $0.99 e-book, I would have recommended that you find yourself a room with no windows and lots of padding.

But in that intervening year, I did a lot of investigating into what other people had written about their BookBub promotions, in addition to studying BookBub's own reported statistics and recommendations.

My conclusion:
Ninety-nine cents is the new free.

Yes, it costs significantly more to advertise a $0.99 book than a free book, and yes, you will see far fewer downloads. However, you stand a much better chance of recouping your advertising costs by promoting a $0.99 book than by offering it free and then praying to All That Is Holy that people will also choose to buy your sequels and other books.

The advice I read from other authors suggested combining a BookBub feature with advertising on other sites, which I decided to follow.

The promos I chose to run for *Dawnflight* in conjunction with BookBub's feature deal, set for a day or more later to gauge the first day of the BookBub promo by itself, included BookSends (http://booksends.com/advertise.php), Books Butterfly's "Titanium 30" option (http://www.booksbutterfly.com/order/paidbook-slots/), eBookSoda (http://www.ebooksoda.com/authors/), Genre Pulse (http://www.genrepulse.com/how-it-works/), and around twenty other free email sites scheduled using the KDROI web browser app, for a total cost of $482.00, not counting the KDROI onetime download fee of $39.00 that I had paid several months earlier.

A leap of faith? Oh, you bet.

Would I have snagged more downloads had I offered *Dawnflight* free? Oh, you bet. Thousands if not tens of thousands more. However, would I have recouped the promo cost by the sales of other books in the series?

With only one full-length sequel, one partial sequel, and two spinoff novellas available at the time, I'm not altogether certain I would have. Most people downloading a free book will add it to the hundreds of other free books on their e-readers, and heaven only knows when they will get around to reading mine. Customers who have purchased a book, even at only $0.99, will be more likely to read it sooner.

Important: Make sure your best work is what you're

discounting, whether it's for $0.99 or free. It could be a reader's first introduction to your work, and you don't want to squander that lone golden chance to make a great first impression.

With BookBub, you must first impress their curators; the jurying process is thorough and rigorous. Offer your audience a taste of your very best full-length work at $0.99 so you can still profit from the promo.

The burst of speed

IN THE notes that I had made when I learned of *Dawnflight*'s selection, which I share in the "Lessons learned" portion of this section, I reminded myself to start checking for sales after three p.m. ET on the day of the feature.

This estimate was based upon a statement in the BookBub Deal Checklist: "Your deal will go live on our website between 6–9 a.m. PST, and the email will generally be delivered by 10 a.m.–noon PST." (https://www.bookbub.com/partners/checklist).

Still, I couldn't resist taking an early peek. I fired up my KDP dashboard at around eleven fifteen that morning and noticed that I had already logged well over a hundred downloads of *Dawnflight* alone, and its sequels and my stand-alone books were attracting the attention of buyers too. The needle had moved into the respectable range on Nook as well.

In an hour those numbers had doubled, and the counters kept spinning at a dizzying rate throughout the afternoon and evening and well into the night.

Squealing my vocal cords raw

I BROKE even on the BookBub promo investment by eleven p.m., around twelve hours into the feature period.

By the beginning of the next day, when most of the other paid promos were scheduled to begin, I had already broken even on those too.

At last I could let go of the rail and truly enjoy the feel of the wind whipping my hair and slipping past my face and fingers.

The best coasters have lesser, tighter loops and dips to rekindle your squeals as the ride thunders toward its conclusion, and the coaster that is a BookBub promotion for an independently published book is no different.

The first such secondary squeal occurred when I learned that BookBub had placed *Dawnflight* in its top slot for the fantasy category that day. The curators had verified my *USA Today* review blurb and even mined a few more words from it than I usually use.

Although I've had novels hit the top twenty in an Amazon category at a time when I had never heard of BookBub or those other paid promo sites, I never thought I'd see the day when *Dawnflight* and its sequels occupied the top three spots in their category, to say nothing of climbing into the top three hundred of all paid Kindle books or having my Amazon author rank crack the top forty—high enough to have that ranking posted on all my books' product pages that day.

Another minisqueal occurred when I learned about my iBooks sales, since I distribute to that platform via Draft2Digital, where royalty reporting is delayed by as much as two days for Apple and longer for some of the other sales channels.

You may have even heard the whoop I let out when I checked my ACX dashboard and learned that approximately 10 percent of the *Dawnflight* e-book customers had purchased its audiobook edition. That in itself was as great a thrill as the mountain of e-book downloads.

All good things…

IN THE vacuum of space, a body in motion will stay in motion. Here on earth, alas, all bodies are subject to outside forces such as gravity and friction, and hence coasters must roll to a stop. After all, it's time for the next batch of passengers to have their turn.

For as much as three weeks after I had reset *Dawnflight* to its pre-BookBub pricing, all my books logged more downloads per day than they experienced prior to the BookBub feature. That was every bit as thrilling as the initial rush, for it meant I had gained fans who wished to seek out more of my work.

Lessons learned

IF YOU have achieved the Holy Grail of book marketing by landing a BookBub featured promotion, these are the steps you need to take to maximize the return on your investment:

- **IMMEDIATELY:** Decide on how long you want to keep the deal in place. (I recommend no more than five days), confirm your assigned feature date, and pay your invoice. BookBub gives you some leeway in paying, but you don't want to risk getting busy and forgetting. They will cancel your feature if it remains unpaid seven days prior to the assigned date.
- **IMMEDIATELY:** Relay any specific instructions not already conveyed. "Let us know if there's anything in particular we should be aware of about your listing—for instance, if there are multiple editions of the same book available or if the cover has recently changed."

(source: BookBub Deal Checklist, https://www.book-bub.com/partners/checklist).

- **IMMEDIATELY:** If you code your own e-books, begin making sure all embedded product links are up to date for all major platforms (Amazon, Nook, iBooks, etc.), and all available books. If you have several titles and are pressed for time, prioritize as follows: the featured book, other titles in the series, then all your other books.

  If you don't code your own e-books, ask whether your formatter person or company will do this for you, whether they can complete the work at least three days prior to your BookBub feature, and how much those updates will cost.

- **IMMEDIATELY:** Reschedule any upcoming Kindle Unlimited promotions that might adversely impact paid downloads related to the featured book. You're already paying an arm and both legs to feature one book; let your readers have a shot at any free books either before or after the BookBub promotion, not on the same day. My rule of thumb is to wait three days before running another KU free promo.

- **As soon as possible:** Set up free and paid advertising with as many other email promoters as will fit within your budget. You may elect to schedule these promos to kick in a day or more after the BookBub promo to help keep your momentum going. Oftentimes a potential customer will decide to purchase an e-book if it enjoys a decent Amazon rank.

- **TEN days prior:** Drop prices on Nook, the iBooks Store, Smashwords, Kobo, and Google Play (you can schedule the promo on the latter two platforms in advance) for the featured book only. Ask your friends to "report

[the] lower price" to Amazon so that its regular Kindle price gets crossed out in favor of the matched price. This is a marketing trick to help maximize the deal's "wow factor" in the potential customer's mind.

Note: Once you have scheduled your temporary Kobo sale, don't mess with it. I somehow managed to cancel one while trying to double check it, and BookBub removed it from their list of sites to promote, thereby causing me to lose heaven knows how many sales.

- **ONE day prior:** Check the featured book's Amazon product page to see if they have matched the price of Nook, iBooks, Kobo, and other e-tailers. If not, then manually lower the price.
- **DAY of:** Relax. Don't start checking for sales until noon eastern time. Okay, fine. Make that nine a.m. But *relax*!
- **EVENING of:** Start checking Amazon, Barnes & Noble, and Kobo category rankings. Log stats and take screenshots when appropriate. Post the exciting bits on Twitter, Facebook, and other social media platforms to reel in more customers.
- ***X* days after:** Raise prices on all platforms again. *X* is the day after the last day of the deal, decided when your BookBub feature was confirmed.

From the BookBub policies page: "If a partner [i.e., advertiser] expires a deal early with us more than once, we unfortunately will not be able to continue working with them. Please let us know in advance of the promotion if you need to adjust the end date." (https://www.bookbub.com/partners/policies)   Do take that bit of advice seriously if you want to keep drinking from this chalice as often as they'll let you.

For more information

- IF you've heard disturbing rumors, Carlyn Robertson reveals "11 BookBub Myths Busted" on BookBub's blog (http://insights.bookbub.com/bookbub-myths-busted/). Most of the "myths" are fairly commonsense.
- THERE'S an interesting take on BookBub by nonfiction author Mike Alvear in the *Huffington Post* (http://www.huffingtonpost.com/mike-alvear/it-isnt-amazon-publishers_b_8307708.html). Many of the comments are well worth the read too.
- BOOKBUB offers advice on how to maximize one's chances of being accepted: http://insights.bookbub.com/how-bookbub-selection-process-works/.
- ANOTHER article in *BookBub Insights* describes the categories subscribers sign up for: http://insights.bookbub.com/what-else-are-your-bookbub-readers-reading/. It's all pretty much commonsense stuff, but the statistics are interesting if you're into that sort of thing.
- SCOTTISH author Mary Smith relates her success on BookBub with a free-book promo here: http://jackieweger.com/book-promotions-indie-authors-report-results/.
- AMERICAN author Angela Roquet compares her experiences with BookBub advertising for paid versus free-download books on her blog *Roquet's Reapings* (http://angelaroquet.blogspot.com/2016/08/book-bub-promo-comparison-free-vs-99cents.html).

BookBub now offers advertising that's not a featured deal. They present a great infographic of the difference between ads and featured deals in this blog post (https://insights.bookbub.com/bookbub-featured-deals-vs-bookbub-ads-whats-the-difference/). In summary, an ad may describe any book-related content, including audiobooks, print editions, and full-price e-books. It's a new program as of mid-2016, and I am eligible but have not yet begun to participate. The *BookBub Partners* blog, however, offers one author's case study for your consideration: https://insights.bookbub.com/promoting-a-box-set-with-bookbub-ads-case-study/.

My final BookBub lesson to impart to you

DON'T SHY from selecting international promotion when submitting your book's deal for consideration, even though it's less expensive to do so.

When my medieval paranormal novel *Snow in July* was selected only for BookBub's non-US email lists (UK, Canada, Australia, and India), I still was able to recoup my BookBub investment within the first twenty-four hours even though this novel is a stand-alone, Barnes & Noble had just shut down its non-US Nook websites, and far fewer customers bought my other novels or audiobooks.

The other advantage to accepting an international-only BookBub promotion is that they waive the six-month repeat advertising restriction for the title in question, and you may submit it for US promotion consideration again in as little as one month. I did this for *Snow in July*, and I was thrilled when they selected it for US promotion less than two months after its international BookBub debut. To improve its chances for selection, I made sure to mention that its sales performance during the international-only promotion exceeded by almost double BookBub's reported average download numbers for the teen and young adult category.

One last note on the statistics: don't be discouraged if your book doesn't meet that coveted "average downloads" number. As my husband the stats professor will be the first to point out, the average of any data set is skewed by outliers (i.e., rogue data points that lie far above or below the norm). In the case of BookBub's reported download averages, the values are skewed high because of reports by authors of *New York Times* and *USA Today* best-selling books who advertise in that venue. Authors whose books didn't perform as well as the reported average will very likely choose not to participate in the postadvertising survey, further skewing the results toward the high side.

A more accurate statistic to report to potential advertisers for comparison purposes is the median—the value of the middle data point of the set—which is unaffected by outliers, since each data point is given equal weight regardless of its value. This is something I mention on every BookBub survey I submit, and I will continue to mention it until they change their reporting policy. It would be helpful for everyone if you can join me in this crusade.

4G. Offering Something for Nothing: How to Create a Permafree Title

NINETY-NINE CENTS MAY be the new free, but I haven't yet met a reader who doesn't like free books, so there is wisdom in offering one or more of your e-books free in perpetuity, or "permafree."

Making a print book available for free is as simple as donating copies to libraries; with digital editions it's a bit trickier, given that the largest e-book distributor on the planet, Amazon, does not let you specify a $0.00 price for your e-books using your vendor account.

You can circumvent that limitation by distributing your title to Kindle via Smashwords, which will allow you to set a $0.00 for all sales channels. If you're like me and prefer to use Draft2Digital, which no longer allows distribution to Kindle, you can still achieve Amazon's price matching for your permafree title by completing these steps:

1. DISENROLL your e-book from Kindle Unlimited, if you haven't already, and wait until its current exclusivity period ends before you publish it on any other retail platforms or you will incur the wrath of Amazon. You do not want to incur the wrath of Amazon; trust me.
2. PUBLISH it on Nook, Kobo, and Smashwords, where you can set a price of $0.00 using your vendor account.
3. IF you have a vendor account on the iBooks Store and they will let you set a $0.00 price, please let me know.

Lacking any Apple hardware, I publish to the iBooks Store via Draft2Digital.

4. GET yourself a vendor account at Smashwords and Draft2Digital. Here you can set a $0.00 price for your e-book and distribute it to the aforementioned iBooks Store plus Nook and Kobo (if you'd rather not maintain a separate vendor account on those platforms), Scribd, Inktera/Page Foundry, and some European distributors such as 24Symbols and Tolino. I get a lot of downloads of my free Spanish and German titles through Tolino, and on occasion I score paid downloads of the other translated books via those sales channels too.

5. ONCE you have verified that the $0.00 prices are in effect at all the other e-tailers' sites, visit the Amazon product page for your book and report the lower price using the link popup located below your book's sales rankings. Get your friends to do the same for you; the more reports Amazon receives, the faster the price matching will get activated.

6. IF for some reason Step 5 fails to achieve the desired result, email Amazon and ask them to price match the title. Author Clare Flynn reported the success of the email tactic in this blog post on the *Self-Publishing Advice Center* blog (http://selfpublishingadvice.org/book-marketing-how-and-why-to-make-a-self-published-book-permafree/).

I caution you, however, to offer only your very best work free, because this title is going to be your ambassador to potential new fans of your work, and you only get that one golden chance to make a good first impression.

The title you choose to offer free does not have to

be a full-length novel. My permafree title, *The Color of Vengeance*, is a novella excerpted from a much longer work, *Morning's Journey*. I'm sure *The Color of Vengeance* would get more downloads if it was a longer work; therefore, I plan to set up the first book in the series, *Dawnflight*, as permafree eventually too.

Whatever the book's length, make sure it contains links to all your other books and their available editions.

Some e-tailers such as Nook permit the embedding of YouTube videos in the EPUB file, making it easy to attract customers to other titles in your backlist by displaying their book trailers. Do include the hyperlink to the trailers' YouTube pages as a backup method for accessing them, however. During the upload and conversion process at KDP, the <iframe> HTML embed code gets stripped out regardless of whether you have uploaded an EPUB or a MOBI file. I have elected to keep the <iframe> code in my e-books' files, however, in case that policy ever changes.

If you are unsure what I mean by the <iframe> code but have uploaded your book trailer to YouTube, visit the trailer's YouTube page, click the "Share" link, click on the "Embed" tab, and then copy the line that appears highlighted by default. It starts with "<iframe>" and ends with "</iframe>." This line gets pasted into your e-book's HTML code at the location you wish for the trailer to be displayed.

Caution: You must delete the "allowfullscreen" attribute from the <iframe> code that YouTube generates because EPUBCheck (http://validator.idpf.org/), the software employed by all e-book distributors to validate your EPUB file after you've uploaded it, does not permit that attribute to appear in EPUB files and will generate an error upon encountering it.

4H. Offering till It Hurts: Using Giveaways to Market Your Book

SHORTLY AFTER *DAWNFLIGHT* was published by Simon & Schuster in 1999, I was attending a meeting of the Washington Romance Writers, where I heard a fellow first-time author gush that she loved giving away copies of her book.

My internal monologue:

Loved? Really?? But what about the lost sales???

I have lived and learned, and now the older and wiser me is here to instruct you.

All together, class: What is the purpose of marketing?

To increase exposure for you and your book.

Is that the answer you came up with? Good. Now you're getting it.

Any sales that may result from your marketing efforts, including giveaways, are pure gravy.

There are several ways to set up book-related give-aways, which include:

- **AMAZON.** To get started, go to your book's product page and look for the "Set up an Amazon Giveaway" head-ing beneath the customer reviews summary or forum discussions. If you don't see that heading on the main product page, then your book doesn't qualify. If you publish and distribute all your books via Lightning

Source or IngramSpark, you're out of luck on this option; keep scrolling for giveaway options you can exercise.

Amazon gives you several choices from which to select your call to action for customers to enter your giveaway, but I recommend selecting "Follow on Amazon" for three reasons:

1. AMAZON customers don't usually unfollow an author after the contest is over, as they might on Twitter and other social media platforms.
2. YOU acquire more people whom Amazon will automatically email about your new releases and price drops.
3. THE Amazon follows boost your author rank.

YOU may set up Amazon giveaways for e-books as well as print books.

THE biggest drawback to Amazon's giveaways for print editions, however, is that you must purchase your book's copies at full retail price, not at your much-lower print-on-demand printing cost, and you must pay an astronomical amount—up front—in potential shipping costs, based on the assumption that all copies will be awarded. They refund the amount, including shipping, of all unawarded copies to your credit card, and the final cost of awarded copies is mitigated by the royalties earned, but the price for setting up the giveaway can give you a severe case of sticker shock.

YOU have the option with unawarded e-books to either set up a new giveaway or download the corresponding number of gift codes to be distributed at your discretion; the refund option is not available for e-books.

To view your Amazon giveaway dashboard, sign on to your Amazon account and then follow this link: https://www.amazon.com/giveaway/host/dashboard.

- **GOODREADS.** Jenn Hanson-dePaula on the *Mixtus Media* blog talks about ways to use Goodreads to expand your audience, including Goodreads give-aways (http://mixtusmedia.com/blog/how-to-use-goodreads-to-dramatically-grow-your-audience). Goodreads giveaways are for physical copies of your book rather than e-books or audio downloads, and a giveaway's sponsor cannot specify a call to action as a requirement for entry. However, with Goodreads you get the advantage that the majority of entrants—if not already fans of yours—are at least avid book readers. Furthermore, authors are no longer restricted to set-ting up giveaways for books that have been released for less than one year. That said, more entrants can gener-ally be expected for a giveaway featuring a newer title.

I have netted several reviews and star rank-ings of my books via Goodreads giveaways. Winners are never required to post a review, but many do. You must pay postage costs, which may be lessened by limiting entrants to your home country, but it's a tax-deductible expense.

If you have at least one published book to your credit—or if you are in the process of writing your first book—you may learn how to become a Goodreads author here: https://www.goodreads.com/author/

program.

- **LIBRARYTHING.** I have not yet availed myself of the option to set up giveaways using LibraryThing, and I need to try it. If you are a designated LibraryThing Author, or if you have more than fifty books logged in your LibraryThing account, or if you have a paid LibraryThing account, you are eligible to set up member giveaways. Complete information may be viewed here: http://www.librarything.com/wiki/index.php/HelpThing:Er_list#How_do_I_give_away_books_with_the_Member_Giveaways_program.3F.

  More information for authors, including how to become a LibraryThing Author, may be viewed on this page: http://www.librarything.com/about_authors.php.

- **RAFFLECOPTER.** The sky's the limit for prizes that can be specified within Rafflecopter, including swag, gift cards, and books of any type of edition, and you can specify multiple prize tiers wherein some winners are chosen from the international pool of entrants and some are limited to a specified country of origin. I exercise this option via virtual blog tours, though Rafflecopter's free service level may fit most authors' needs.   (https://www.rafflecopter.com/pricing)

  Another advantage to a Rafflecopter giveaway is that you can structure it to give entrants more than one opportunity to win, such as subscribing to your blog or newsletter, following you on various social media platforms, and sending out a specific tweet. That's the meaning of the "/number" in the top right corner of the Rafflecopter widget—the number of entry opportunities available for you to exercise in the given contest.

I also run my own monthly giveaways from the pool of people who have followed me on various social media platforms and who have commented upon my blog posts. In these types of contests, I have found the website Random.org (https://www.random.org/) invaluable for impartially choosing a winner.

Another technique I've implemented with fantastic results is **creating print editions** of my short stories, each one in a separate booklet. I publish these via CreateSpace, where I obtain a free CreateSpace-assigned ISBN and use their Cover Creator template, which allows me to upload the e-book's cover. Each story costs me less than $2.50 per copy, delivered. Distributing these at personal appearances has resulted in digital downloads as well as sales of my full-length books' print editions.

CreateSpace—and its Kindle Direct Publishing counterpart, KDP Print—imposes the limitation that your booklet's interior file must be at least twenty-four pages. That's not hard to achieve with a five-thousand-word story when you select the smallest industry-standard trim size (5" x 8"), set ample (but not ridiculously so) margins and gutters, include a title page, a copyright page, and (if appropriate) a page of review blurbs in the frontmatter section, and in the backmatter you display information about your backlist along with your author bio.

Giving away stand-alone short stories sidesteps the issue of potentially alienating your audience by publishing the first chapter or two of a much longer book. It's one of the first questions I get asked whenever I mention my freebies, and my answer always wins a grin from my booth's visitors. This marketing practice creates a high instance of their returning to purchase my other books, and sometimes that even happens right on the spot.

Furthermore, these CreateSpace-generated booklets are eligible as Amazon giveaway prizes.

I've stated this before and I'll state it again: make sure that you're creating giveaway samples of your best writing. You will never get another chance with that reader to make a good first impression.

Book contests are a specialized form of giveaway, and I am pleased to report that most of my books have been nominated for or have won regional, national, and international contests. Contests are considered giveaways because you're providing free digital or print copies of your books to the judges or to a local library of the contest administrator's choosing. It can be difficult to pinpoint specific sales to a contest win, however, so I urge you to exercise caution when deciding upon which contests to enter. There are many from which to choose, they exist at all points of the cost and respectability spectrum, and they will chew up your marketing budget in a heartbeat if you're not careful.

Book reviews may be considered giveaways too, since you are providing copies to potential reviewers free of charge. Later in this chapter I give advice on how to wrangle this particular beast.

4I. Not Your Mama's Book's Media Kit

B EFORE DELVING INTO the topic of obtaining reviews for your book, I wish to touch on the preparatory subject of its media kit, since you may need something of this nature to send to book reviewers.

A media kit is a collection of materials an author assembles to inform journalists and—these days—bloggers and tour coordinators about their books for promotional purposes.

When I began my publishing career in 1999, the media kit was a two-pocket folder assembled to exacting specifications.

In the left pocket, front to back, were tucked the author's photo, contact information and bio, and any prior publications and awards.

The right pocket contained the most recent release's cover flat (publisher jargon referring to the marketing tool produced by large traditional publishers that consisted of the print book's wrap cover with selling points printed on the back). Behind the cover flat were tucked sheets that included the book's information such as genre, release date, series title if applicable, and retail price; tagline and synopsis; and any available press releases and reviews.

If you plan to attend major conventions or other events where reporters are expected, it's not a bad idea to carry a physical media kit.

The age of virtual book tours has prompted the metamorphosis of the media kit to digital form, including the aforementioned author and book information, along with, where available:

- AUTHOR'S (and publisher's, if applicable) website link
- PUBLICATION history if an older release, including previous title and publisher as applicable
- MAJOR thematic elements such as "vampires," "shapeshifters," "May-December romance," and so forth
- SUGGESTED audience rating (PG, R, etc.), or "heat level" if a romance ("mild," "steamy," "keep a jug of water handy," "roll out the fire hose")
- LINKS to YouTube interviews
- PURCHASE links for alternative editions such as paperback, hardcover, and audiobook
- BOOK trailers (links as well as embed codes)
- LINKS to award announcements
- A list of the author's social media accounts to follow
- SAMPLE chapter
- EXCERPTS
- TEASER graphics
- ANIMATED book cover GIF files
- STATIC cover graphics
- COLLECTIONS of sample tweets
- LINKS to e-tailer author pages

Some authors prefer to assemble one media kit that describes all of their books. If your collection contains more than three books, however, you might be wise to consider establishing a separate media kit for each book or series. This makes it easy to approach bloggers who might be interested in running a spotlight of one of your books on their blogs.

If you employ blog-tour companies, more than likely they will send you their media kit format. Ask them, as a professional courtesy, whether it's acceptable to substitute the media kit you have already prepared.

4J. On the Hunt for Book Reviews

Have you ever bought a new car and then suddenly you're seeing "your" car all over the road? That's what happened to me when I decided to blog about book reviews. Suddenly bloggers were driving "my" topic all over the information superhighway!

It's a good thing that there's plenty of room for all of us.

4J1. The Importance of Book Reviews

If you have even one title in a retail catalog, then more than likely you have noticed the fluctuation in sales in response to receiving a new review. Instinctively we authors know that reviews are important, but longtime author Gail Z. Martin offers an interesting perspective about why in her guest blog post on *No Wasted Ink* (http://nowastedink.com/2015/07/17/guest-post-why-reader-reviews-matter-by-gail-z-martin/).

4J2. Reacting to Reviews

The first review I ever got for the first edition of *Dawnflight* in 1999 I received via email from the reviewer. I think I must have stared at the subject line for at least an hour, terrified to open it. But I'm glad I did, for the review was a glowing one.

Since then my books have received dozens of reviews,

falling at all points across the starry spectrum, and for numerous reasons.

You know how to handle the 5- and 4-star reviews, right? Since chances are I'm old enough to be your mom, I will do my Mom Thing and make sure you know: be gracious and humble. And then tweet/pin/share the bejezus out of them.

I've found 3-star reviews of my books to be a mixed bag of anything from ripping my book a new one to containing far more praise than the star rating would seem to indicate. Sometimes I find tweetable tidbits in these reviews and sometimes not. Either way, I read them and then go about my day.

But how should one react to the 2- and 1-star wonders?

Alan Kealey, news editor at *Indie Author News*, gives an excellent list of tips in "10 Ways for Authors to Respond to Bad Reviews" (http://www.indieauthornews.com/2015/03/10-ways-for-authors-to-handle-bad-book-reviews.html). My number-one tip, which is his number two:

> Never interact with reviewers in a public forum regardless of the review's content or star rating. Ever. Period.

If you believe that rules are made to be broken, the only exception to this rule you should consider is to post a thank-you, even in response to a low-star-rating review if it contains constructive criticism that you find useful for improving your work. A little courtesy goes a long way.

And do not—ever, exclamation point—badger a

reviewer because she or he had the audacity to rate your book fewer than five stars. This happened to me. My review (as always) contained my reasons for knocking one point off the maximum, I further explained my reasons to the author in a private email exchange but she would have none of it... and I'll never read another book by that author again, even for free. Yes, you read that right: I got yelled at for rating a book four stars rather than five. Don't act like that author, please.

4J3. Review Swapping

AUTHOR TRACI Sanders published an excellent blog post about writing reviews for Amazon that takes into consideration their campaign to weed out "fake" (whether real or imagined by the Amazon bots) reviews. The full article may be viewed on the *A Word With Traci* blog (http://awordwithtraci.com/the-dos-and-donts-of-reviewing-on-amazon/).

As a professional reviewer—and by that I mean that I have been paid cash for my content by the review site, never directly by publishers or authors—I take a dim view of review swapping. This, along with the ethically challenged practice of purchasing reviews, has done more to undermine the value of reviews than coercing your family and friends to leave good reviews ever will.

Do you believe that having a thousand five-star reviews of your book will convince me to buy it? If I recognize your name from a *New York Times* or *USA Today* best-seller list... maybe. Otherwise, I will presume that you have purchased the vast majority of those ratings as a marketing ploy and will move along to the next book on the page.

4.J4. Requesting Reviews

DONE CORRECTLY, this can be a tedious and time-consuming process.

At one point I employed an assistant to work on this project for a few hours per month. I started her with the "Indie Reviewers List" (http://www.theindieview.com/indie-reviewers/) maintained by *The Indie View* and identified the genres wherein each of my books fits. She conducted all the querying, submitting, and following up. The guidelines I gave her will work for you too:

1. PAY attention to what the blogger prefers to read. Don't waste his or her time—or yours—by submitting your book if it doesn't fit unless the blogger specifically states that exceptions are made for exceptional works. When in doubt, proceed to step number two.
2. READ a few posted reviews, especially the negative ones. You may decide that you don't like the reviewer's style, and that could save you and the blogger some time.
3. FOLLOW the reviewer's stated submission guidelines to the letter. If she or he does not want your book's file right away, do not send it. That's the fastest way of getting it dumped—and potentially getting yourself labeled as An Author Who Does Not Read. This goes double for responding to sites that state they are closed to submissions.
4. IF the site is open to submissions but no guidelines exist, write a brief but courteous email giving your book's title, genre(s), and tagline, which ideally describes your book in twenty words or fewer. Don't

waste his or her time (or yours) by including a twenty-page synopsis and a ten-page author bio in addition to your manuscript in its entirety.

When following up with potential reviewers after you have submitted your book:

1. HEED the reviewer's stated follow-up policies to the letter. If she or he specifies "do not contact us" and you contact them anyway, then you run the risk of being labeled as An Author Who Does Not Read.
2. ADD at least one month to any stated follow-up period, if follow-ups are permitted.
3. IF no follow-up guidelines or review-posting turn-around times are stated, and the site has not posted a "do not contact" policy, wait at least three months before following up with the blogger. Reviewer-bloggers are busy people too, and they do not need to be hounded by anyone.

Less daunting, tedious, and time-consuming is the blog tour.

In a properly coordinated tour, potential reviewers might be incentivized to participate by being offered the chance to win a gift card in a bloggers-only giveaway, but they are not compensated financially for writing the review itself, because they are never under any obligation to write it. To protect authors, the usual stipulation is that if a reviewer dislikes the book and cannot rate it more than two stars, the tour coordinator asks that the review not be posted until after the tour is over.

Of course "less daunting, tedious, and time-consuming" equals greater cost—recall that marketing triad of skill, money, and time I mentioned earlier in this chapter—but all of my books have benefited from being featured in blog tours, and I feel that they are marketing dollars well spent.

Another service about which I've heard good reports, though it's far more expensive for individual authors than running blog tours, is NetGalley (https://netgalley. uservoice.com/knowledgebase/topics/16110-for-publishers-and-authors). Some authors mitigate the cost by forming collectives with other authors, though I'm satisfied with the review results I get from blog tours and have not joined any NetGalley communes.

4K. Defining Subject Headings and Keywords, or "My Book is BI-*What*?"

M Y HAIRDRESSER ONCE complimented me on how much weight I had lost after the birth of my first child.

"You look so svelte!" he gushed.

Another of his clients overheard and asked me my secret.

"Diet and exercise," I said.

She looked crestfallen… as if she had expected me to spout some magic formula.

As with losing weight, there is no magic formula for getting your book noticed out of the millions of titles that are published each year. But you may save your crest-fallen face for something that's an everlasting disappointment—US politicians, for example.

In publishing, the right subject headings and keywords can help your work shoot to the top of potential customers' search results pages.

4K1. BISAC Basics

IF YOU'VE spent time defining your book's information in Bowker, CreateSpace, IngramSpark, KDP Print, or any of the e-book vendor accounts, you'll see the acronym BISAC, or Book Industry Standards and Communications. Managed by Book Industry Study Group Inc. (http://bisg.org/), the BISAC Subject Headings is a list of several hundred classifications for identifying a book's subject matter.

Amazon calls this classification the *browse category* and likens it to major headings you'll find labeling the aisles of a brick-and-mortar bookstore. It's an apt analogy.

As of this writing, the BISAC 2016 edition is the most recent list.

For the record, the BISAC category Non-Classifiable (NON000000) applies to books containing no subject matter, such as blank books. It is not intended for use with a book that contains multiple nonfiction topics or elements of many fiction genres.

Some distributors, like Amazon and Draft2Digital, kindly lead you through the selection process by giving you expansion choices when a BISAC subject code (e.g., Fiction, FIC000000) contains subordinate codes. Others, like Google Play, expect you to know the codes off the top of your head... or else you must know where to find the latest list.

I'll save you the headache. The BISAC 2016 edition may be viewed by visiting this page: http://bisg.org/page/BISAC2015Edition. (Pay no mind to the "2015" embedded in the URL. The BISG webmaster updated the page's title for 2016 but not its filename.) If you write fiction, save yourself a click by starting here: http://bisg.org/page/Fiction.

In theory, you may assign as many BISAC codes to your book as you wish. In practice, you must heed each distributor's rules.

Amazon and IngramSpark, for instance, limit a book's BISAC identification to two codes; with Kobo you may choose three. Nook Press, on the other hand, permits the assignment of up to five codes. Most third-party book distributors, such as Draft2Digital, will allow you to assign the maximum number supported by at least one of their partner e-tailers, but they advise you to make your selections in order of importance because not all e-tailers will accept that many BISAC codes for your book.

4K2. Keyword Conundrum

IF BISAC codes are like the bookstore's aisle signs, keywords are what you tell the customer service representative to help you further refine your search of the store's shelves.

I once attended a panel at a science fiction/fantasy convention, where I learned that I could stuff the "seven keywords" field available in KDP with huge multiword phrases.

The phrases don't even have to make sense as long as the words are applicable to the book and don't violate Amazon's keyword rules such as using a celebrity's name to imply an endorsement.

This was exciting news, since most of my novels contain elements from several genres, and redefining their keywords became one of the first tasks I assayed after I got home from the convention.

What the presenter neglected to mention, however, was the 350-character limit that I bumped up against in KDP. The keyword limit is even shorter in CreateSpace— five keywords of no more than twenty-five characters apiece. In Nook Press you're limited to just one hundred characters total, including commas and spaces.

Still, you are doing yourself and your book a favor by stuffing in as many keywords as each e-book publishing platform allows.

Not sure where to start?

Amazon's article "Make Your Book More Discoverable with Keywords" (https://kdp.amazon.com/help?topicId=A2EZES9JAJ6H02) is a good best-practices reference and contains their recommended dos and don'ts. Another general reference, "Selecting Browse Categories," (https://kdp.amazon.com/help?topicId=A200PDG-PEIQX41) includes links to keyword tables by Amazon category to help you decide how to land your book in one or more subcategories. A few of the most popular category tables include:

- BIOGRAPHIES & Memoirs (https://kdp.amazon.com/help?topicId=A36KHEOF75R4ON)
- BUSINESS & Money (https://kdp.amazon.com/help?topicId=A29VGOF8XYTB2M)
- COMICS & Graphic Novels (https://kdp.amazon.com/help?topicId=A1ZXLAOYL8FYN4)
- HISTORY (https://kdp.amazon.com/help?topicId=A1TB2YNQH46L8)
- LITERATURE & Fiction (https://kdp.amazon.com/help?topicId=A3O9QROY7AIQG2)
- MYSTERY, Thriller, & Suspense (https://kdp.amazon.com/help?topicId=A3NTX9NCJD3D5X)
- RELIGION & Spirituality (https://kdp.amazon.com/help?topicId=A2LC0L7BXECUP6)
- ROMANCE (https://kdp.amazon.com/help?topicId=A19G4ONBAU6NO3)
- SCIENCE Fiction & Fantasy (https://kdp.amazon.com/help?topicId=A2G3ZMYDPB9VRM)
- TEEN & Young Adult (https://kdp.amazon.com/help?topicId=A1XEN0SRCO1KPB)

Don't be shy about pulling keywords from categories that you might not otherwise think of for your novel, as long as they fit—though it's not a foolproof system. I'm still trying to figure out how my futuristic time-travel political satire, *King Arthur's Sister in Washington's Court*, wound up at the top of Amazon's "Alien Invasion" category during the opening hours of its first BookBub campaign. Just smile and wave, boys, indeed.

Keyword definition is not all fun and games, however. Sarah Arrow contributed an article to the *Sark eMedia* blog (http://www.sarkemedia.com/actions-that-make-keywords-irrelevant/) listing actions that render your keywords less effective. It's geared toward bloggers, but the "Know Your Niche" and "Know your Audience" tips are essential for book authors.

If you're struggling with understanding your audience, Georgina Roy offers "5 Ways to Learn About Your Target Audience for Your Book" (http://e-booksindia.com/5-ways-to-learn-about-your-target-audience-for-your-book/) on the *e-Books India* blog. The title is a bit of a misnomer, since tip number five identifies what an author should do once he or she has exercised tips one through four, but her advice provides a good starting point.

4L. Advice That's Not for the Birds: Twitter Marketing for Authors

EVERY AUTHOR HAS her or his preferred social media platform for promoting, and mine has become Twitter. There are a few reasons for my choice, not the least of which being that a family drama played out on Facebook in the worst way imaginable, forever darkening my impression of that forum. From a promotional standpoint, Facebook's usefulness for free marketing became nullified the instant they changed their display algorithms to kill the concept of organic reach and convince more businesses to pay to boost their posts. Now the best thing for an author to do on that platform is join the ever-expanding list of book-promotion groups where readers may be reached directly and still for free.

Thus endeth my Facebook marketing advice.

Some people believe that you cannot sell books using Twitter, but I have found a direct correlation between certain tweets and sales, and it occurs often enough to convince me to keep my primary promotional activities focused on that platform.

As a general rule, readers will not take a chance on buying the work of a new-to-them author until they have seen mention of the book or author at least seven times. Twitter is great for improving those odds, especially if you can build a network of faithful retweeters.

Even when a tweet doesn't result in a sale, it can achieve increased click-throughs to your author page or your book's product page. This exposure is what marketing is all about.

When I blogged about this topic, I headlined the post "7 Dos and Don'ts of Twitter Marketing for Authors."

I start with the "Don'ts" because I'm contrary that way.

4L1. Don't...

1. **DON'T assume that there is any privacy in Twitter**, even in direct messages. Structure your tweets and DMs as if you're broadcasting them to the entire universe, including your mom. This isn't strictly marketing, but you can damage your author brand if you tweet something that you didn't want being seen by God and everyone.

2. **DON'T start a tweet with someone's Twitter handle** (@whatever), because the tweet will be seen only by you, @whatever, and mutual followers of you and @whatever. Inserting a single character (a period is a common convention) in front of the @ will increase your tweet's reach many times over. Most of the time I try to start the tweet with a word of thanks or other type of greeting. Even when it's an automated tweet, it lends an air of personalization, and personal interaction is key to closing the deal with a potential customer.

   Note: Even though Twitter now allows a user to retweet his or her own tweets, inserting a character in front of the @whatever is still a great tactic for increasing the organic reach of the original tweet.

3. **DON'T #use #hashtags #too #much #in #your #tweets.** It's annoying as #hell and can make the

tweet hard to read depending on your Twitter profile's display settings. And #don't punctuate #hashtags because that creates something you #didn't intend ("#don," "#hash," and "#didn," for example). You can, however, take advantage of this functionality to punctuate your Twitter handle, creating tweets like:

Read @KimHeadlee's books because they're fantastic!

Note: An underscore ("_") character may be used to separate words in a hashtag; for example, #Be_the_story (https://twitter.com/search?q=%23be_the_story), but that can be more trouble than mashing the words together, as in #BeTheStory (https://twitter.com/search?q=%23bethestory). Those two examples produce different Twitter searches. However, Twitter searches are not case sensitive, so #BETHESTORY, #BeTheStory, and #bethestory yield the same results.

4. **DON'T tweet or retweet exclusively information about your books.** That gets real boring real fast. Bored followers are not engaged followers, and they sure as #hell won't stick around long enough to buy your book.

5. **DON'T send out automated** "Buy my book" / "Like my Facebook page" / "Connect with me on LinkedIn" / "Anything else" **direct messages to new followers.** Twitter's DM system is clunky and too annoying to live, especially with the lifting of the length restrictions. I rarely unfollow anyone for sending me an unsolicited DM, whether automated or not, but I most certainly will never buy your book / like your Facebook page / connect with you on LinkedIn / anything else just because you commanded me to do so in

your DM. And if you insist on keeping your automated "welcome" DM, go ahead and keep it long-winded too. That's an automated guarantee that I won't read any of it as I activate the "leave conversation" function.

6. **DON'T automatically follow everyone who has followed you** just because it's convenient, you want to reduce follower churn (i.e., the number of accounts that unfollow yours if you don't follow them back), and you're pressed for time. That can lead to some very questionable content showing up in your Twitter feed or DM inbox. As a rule, I do not follow:

   - ANYONE who offers to sell me followers on any platform
   - ANY account where either the profile or cover picture looks creepy or stalker-y
   - ANY account that has not yet tweeted anything
   - ANY account wherein all the tweets beg for money
   - ANY account that doesn't tweet at least something in English
   - ANYONE whose account's "about" statement, tweets, or retweets violate my ethical code

   IT's a rare day when I look at my Twitter feed anymore; I usually go straight to notifications and start retweeting from there. Even so, I don't want questionable content in my feed or as an excuse for someone to send me yet another unsolicited DM begging for something from me.

7. **DON'T use common handles** (such as @amazon) **or hashtags** (such as #Kindle) **in your tweets.** The former is an utter waste of tweet space because nobody monitoring @amazon is going to care about your lone tweet, let alone retweet it, and your book will

get lost in the ginormous pile of #Kindle-tagged (or #romance-tagged, etc.) tweets in about four nano-seconds. The object is to go for hashtag unique-ness. Check out #KASIWC (https://twitter.com/search?q=%23kasiwc) if you have any question about how well this technique works.

4L2. Do…

1. **Do check out a new follower's profile.** If appropri-ate, retweet something of theirs or send him/her/it a direct tweet (just keep in mind Don't number two, above), and then follow the account back, because the more accounts you follow, the faster your following will grow. I admit this can be time-consuming, how-ever, and antsy people may unfollow you if you don't follow them in half a heartbeat, but in case you haven't noticed, there are plenty of birds in the Twitterverse sky. And the antsy people may follow you again any-way, especially if your content is worth following. For the record, I try to check my followers list once a day, usually in the evening (eastern time), so if you have followed my @KimHeadlee Twitter account, please be patient; I'll get to you. You shouldn't be antsy as a writer anyway.

2. **Do engage with your followers whenever appro-priate**, and perhaps include a link to your book or author page if they have left clues in their profiles, tweets, or retweets indicating that they might be interested in your work. Failure to perform this bit of basic research and social media etiquette can cause you to run the risk of being branded as a spammer by having too many users block your account, or they

might lodge complaints about you to Twitter support.

3. **Do set up worldwide Amazon links for your books and author page** to increase your odds of landing foreign sales. A great site for this is BookLinker (http://booklinker.net/), because they allow you to specify your own Amazon Associates ID for any business unit where you might have one (United States, United Kingdom, Canada, and so forth). I do get a fair number of affiliate sales that way, and you can too.

Hot Tip: Set up a universal link for all digital editions of your e-book on Books2Read (https://books-2read.com/), be it published on Amazon, Nook, Kobo, or any of the many other online retailers they support. Books2Read is just getting started, however, so they don't yet offer functionality to set up universal links for your author pages, audiobooks, and other types of editions. As BookLinker does with Amazon, Books2Read will allow you to specify your affiliate IDs for all e-tailer platforms.

4. **Do include balanced content in your tweets**, such as blog posts about hobbies and pictures that interest you, other writers' tips, and so forth. A great way to do this, if you blog, is by setting up a free account at Triberr and then becoming a member of "tribes" of like-minded bloggers. Within the first six months of joining, my daily blog views increased one hundredfold. Now I am a member of more than fifty tribes not including my own, I have more than one thousand tribemates (i.e., other bloggers to potentially share my posts), and I enjoy a combined Twitter network reach of twenty-one million (solo, my Twitter follower list is pushing nineteen thousand at present). I

don't care how bad you think you are at math, that's a *lot* of increased exposure.

5. **Do set up cross-posting to Twitter** with your blog, Facebook, Pinterest, and other social media platforms. This is another way to vary your content.

6. **Do establish a free account at Crowdfire or other such tool** that allows you to easily manage your follower and following lists. My personal preference is to unfollow anyone who has unfollowed me the instant I follow them.

7. **Do establish a free account at Hootsuite or other such tool** for scheduling tweets. If using Hootsuite, save all your tweets as drafts so you can tweet them again using Hootsuite's link shortener. My personal rule of thumb is to schedule one of my canned, book-related tweets per hour.

If you have hundreds of reusable tweets, as I do, then I also recommend backing them up. I maintain a spreadsheet with separate tabs (worksheets) for each book plus one for other tweets such as my author profile and website pages, and my newsletter signup link. Each worksheet includes a date and time column corresponding with the date and time I created the draft tweet in Hootsuite so I can find it more easily when I want to change it or use it, and a separate column for the associated link. This format also makes my tweet layout compatible with the Hootsuite Pro bulk message scheduler. You may view my technical advice about that tool on *The Maze*: https://kimiversonheadlee.blogspot.com/2016/08/the-business-of-writing-using-hootsuite.html.

Other social media management services are available (Tweet Jukebox, for example), but Hootsuite is joined at Twitter's hip and doesn't appear to be going away anytime soon. I've done the third-party-app route, and I have way too many tweets to risk going with a tool that might be shut down without notice or forethought. Having Hootsuite chop a character off the "allowed" limit for plain text in scheduled tweets that include a link—without notice, and in spite of the fact that Twitter did not impose that change upon any user accounts—was annoying enough.

There are a few other Twitter marketing trends I've noticed, such as quoting (read, "hijacking") someone's tweet to include a link to your unrelated content. Sometimes I retweet those and sometimes I don't, depending on how many of those I get in my notifications, how annoyed I am either by the hijack itself or if one of my cats has just crash-landed on top of me, and whether Jupiter is aligned with Mars.

Another Twitter marketing trend is the automated "welcome" tweet that contains a book link or teaser graphic. Given a choice between receiving an automated DM and an automated "welcome" tweet, I much prefer the latter—and the vast majority of DMs I receive get deleted unread—but whether or not I retweet your welcome tweet depends upon its content and if I can use it to help balance the content of my Twitter output. Usually I'm happy to do so, but there have been exceptions.

A bonus "do" just for this book
Do MAKE use of the "pinned tweet" option to highlight your newest release, boost awareness of an older book, promote an audiobook edition, garner blog-tour hosts, advertise a giveaway, and so forth.

As with most social-media marketing techniques,

there are no hard-and-fast rules governing pinned tweets beyond the limitations imposed by Twitter upon all tweets, but here are my recommendations:

- IF you're promoting a product page, select a tweet containing an e-tailer link that displays the book's cover. Amazon, Audible, and iBooks links work well for this.
- ADD your book's cover to the tweet if the e-tailer doesn't automatically do it for you. If you have an animated GIF cover or eye-catching meme (whether animated or not), add that instead. Twitter no longer counts images against the tweet's length restriction.
- CHANGE your pinned tweet every so often. I run my Twitter campaigns for about a month. Twitter is all about freshness of content; at three months, a pinned tweet begins to adopt the aroma of back-of-the-fridge leftovers. An older pinned tweet also can give the impression of an inactive Twitter account, which could cost you potential followers. And for heaven's sake, don't feed people stale information such as expired sale deals or signup periods that have ended.
- USE language designed to entice the reader to click the link. At a loss for how to create enticing tweets? Keep reading!

4L3. Writing Better Tweets for Your Books

IF YOU'RE just getting started with your Twitter account, you can read some solid general tweeting advice (if a bit dated, since Twitter has abandoned its longer-tweet plan, and thank heaven for that mercy) by Teena Thach for the *Socedo* blog (http://blog.socedo.com/

how-140-characters-can-stand-out-on-twitter/).

Teena Thach's post describing the mid-2016 Twitter changes—the ability to retweet one's own tweets, the fact that attached images no longer count against the 140-character limit, and so forth—may be viewed here: http://blog.socedo.com/twitters-new-140-character-updates-and-how-to-take-advantage-of-it/. Most of it is sound advice, but I maintain that keeping the character(s) in front of the Twitter handle in a reply to another user is still a valid tactic for increasing the original tweet's organic reach.

For those of you who have been around the Twitter block a time or two, I invite you to consider the following examples.

Tweet example 1

> Wil's Winter: Five Years Later (Red Summer Book 2) Antoinette Houston (Author) http://ow.ly/10... @1975Okame

Does that tweet induce you to click on the book's link? Maybe, if you're already a fan of the series or are familiar with the author's other work.

A better approach is to aim for a unique, intriguing hook, such as:

> Even a small town with a stupid name like Horsenose can have big-city drama. WIL'S WINTER: 5 Yrs Later by @1975Okame https://books2read.com/WilsWinter-by-AntoinetteHouston-ebook

Note that I had to shorten the subtitle and didn't have room for the author's name. I prefer to embed my Twitter handle, @KimHeadlee, in my tweets whenever I have room for it so I can track its reach. But I was fortunate enough—thanks to the kindness of another Kim Headlee who had just gotten married, was contemplating a new Twitter handle, and recalled the "famous author" (her label as well as her offer kept me smiling for a week)—to adopt a handle that's recognizable as my name.

The other issue with the first tweet in example one is that the shortened link expands to point to the paperback edition of the book rather than the Kindle edition I coded into my version. That's not a Twitter sin, per se, but I've learned that most customers will be more likely to impulse buy the less expensive digital version rather than paying far more to kill a tree. And they are less likely to make that extra click to switch from the print edition's product page to that of the digital edition.

Note also that I didn't bother to shorten my link. That's because Twitter dedicates twenty-three characters to a link regardless of its length. Link-shortening software (e.g., Bitly and Hootsuite's embedded link-shortening function) can never free up characters in the tweet. The only reasons to use shortened links:

1. You plan to reuse the tweet, and the shortened link provides the requisite uniqueness
2. You wish to mask the fact that the link includes an affiliate tag

Tweet example 2

> A romantic comedy adventure for anyone who likes a good story. @kezzamac http://ow.ly/10... #beezeebooks

Okay... so we have a romantic comedy-adventure story. What's the title? This tweet leaves thirty-one characters in which to give the title. Potential customers need to see an item at least seven times before deciding to buy it. They won't know what to buy if you don't tell them.

Tweet example 3

> INVISIBLE CHILD is about a boy who is hidden and then abandoned by parents @GolondrinaBooks http://amzn.to/1U...

When I see passive voice in a tweet I wonder whether the book was written that way too. To solve that problem I would rewrite the tweet as:

> What made the parents of @GolondrinaBooks's INVISIBLE CHILD hide and then abandon him? How did he survive? http://amzn.to/1U...

Or:

> What happened to @GolondrinaBooks's abandoned INVISIBLE CHILD? http://amzn.to/1U...

Note that in both cases I reworded the hook as one

or more questions that cannot be answered by either yes or no.

The yes-or-no question is the weakest form of writing because it's the easiest to dismiss. You do not want to give potential readers any excuse to dismiss your books. They are quite adept at making up their own.

Of course, you can also incorporate review blurbs and excerpts in your tweets; I do that with many of my reusable tweets.

In every case, select language designed to entice your readers. The longer you can keep a potential customer engaged with your product, the better the odds of landing the sale.

4M. Waxing Technical, Part 2: Creating and Using QR Codes for Your Book

THE BEST MARKETING content offers potential custom-ers a way to buy the product straight off the adver-tisement, and the quick response code is a great way to capture those impulse buys.

4M1. What Is a QR Code?

A QR code is a specialized bar code readable by smart-phones and other scanning devices. The bar code can contain text, URLs, email addresses, telephone numbers, or any other alphanumeric data.

The smartphone must have a QR reader app installed, and there are several good, free apps available for iPhones, Android devices, and other types of smartphones. My reader of choice is the QR Droid app.

A QR code will never expire as long as the associated link remains valid.

4M2. How to Create a QR Code

EVEN MORE plentiful are the websites that pop up when you perform an Internet search on "free QR code gener-ator." My favorite free QR code generator site is QR Stuff (http://www.qrstuff.com/). Here you can enter any URL—for example, your book's worldwide Amazon link created using BookLinker or other such service, or the Audible link to its audiobook edition—and the site will display the bar code for you to download and use.

There are some book-specific QR code generator sites, such as Relinks.me (http://relinks.me/), but they are limited to products in the Amazon retail catalog, and they will append their Amazon affiliate ID to your book's URL. If you don't have an Amazon affiliate ID, then using Relinks.me will save you the step of creating a worldwide link prior to requesting its QR code, but you must manually set up QR codes for your book's Nook and other e-tailer product pages.

The QR Stuff site offers a subscription service if you want specialty items such as scalable graphics, or if you believe your dynamic (i.e., link-shortened) QR codes will receive more than one thousand user scans per month. If all you're doing is setting up a static link to, for example, your book's Kindle product page, then no limits apply to either the creation or use (scanning) of the free QR codes.

If you want to get fancy, you can embed your own branding graphic by using QR Stuff's partnership with Visuallead (http://visuallead.com). However, if you don't want your customers to be subjected to the company's ads—over which you have no control—Visuallead's ad-free version costs a minimum of $6.25 per month. I thought I might try embedding my imprint graphic for Pendragon Cove Press but decided that the cool factor wasn't worth the monthly subscription cost, and I have no intention of submitting any of my readers to the extra advertising.

4M3. How to Use a QR Code

THE OUTPUT of sites such as QR Stuff and Relinks.me is either a JPG or PNG file that may be embedded in any other image, email, website, or publication. I have placed QR codes on promotional postcards and inside teaser booklets, in the backmatter of my free print editions of *The Challenge* and *The Color of Vengeance*, and even on designs uploaded to DiscountMugs (https://www.discountmugs.com) for screening onto tote bags.

In every case, the key is to make sure there is a high contrast between the QR code graphic and its surrounding background; otherwise, the scan will need to be done in the brightest possible lighting conditions or else it might not work.

I carry a set of promotional cards to most personal appearances, and many of these cards have been designed to display two QR codes: one for the book's trailer on YouTube and the other for its e-book product page. One of my favorite interactions with booth visitors occurs when I use my smartphone to display the book trailer by scanning the QR code on the promo card. It's still a sales technique, but it's a little bit softer—and potentially more appealing—than jumping straight to the buy page.

4N. Book Pricing Strategies, or "A Peck of Pesky Price Points"

H ERE'S A NURSERY rhyme with which to limber your lips:

Peter Author picked a peck of pesky price points...

I could barely type that without garbling it; mega bonus points if you can say it aloud even once!

As the more serious portion of the title suggests, in this section I discuss pricing strategies for print books, as well as for new and older e-books.

4N1. Strategies for Pricing Print Editions

THOUGH MOST independent authors, including myself, release their books in digital format first, I'm going to start with pricing the print edition because this process is fairly straightforward:

1. DETERMINE the per-copy printing and delivery cost. CreateSpace and IngramSpark offer pricing calculators for this purpose. With both print-on-demand companies, you need to know your book's page count, *trim size* (length and width to which interior pages are trimmed), and paper selection (e.g., white paper is the least expensive option) before you can calculate the actual delivered-to-your-door

cost. CreateSpace, however, does not require you to go through the title setup process before giving you access to the printing and shipping calculators. If you know the interior type (black and white or full color, with or without *bleed*), trim size, and number of pages, you can perform printing and shipping estimates using this link: https://www.createspace.com/Products/Book/?sitesearch_query=printing%20cost%20calculator&sitesearch_type=SITE#content7.

Once you navigate to that page, clicking on the "Royalties" tab will display a calculator for determining Amazon royalties based on the book's physical attributes and list price you wish to set. Amazon's ordering and shipping calculators will allow you to view cost trends, based on changing page-count and trim-size parameters, even if you intend to distribute your books using IngramSpark.

2. DETERMINE how many books you will typically order at one time (ten, twenty, one hundred, or some other quantity). If IngramSpark is your company of preference for print-on-demand publishing, you will see the carton quantity for your book once you have completed the setup process and are ready to place your first order.

Note: CreateSpace does not offer volume discounts, but IngramSpark begins offering a price break for orders of one hundred copies or more. This is yet another reason why I prefer printing via IngramSpark.

3. MULTIPLY the printing cost by the number of copies you expect in a typical order, add the shipping cost, and divide by the number of copies to determine your total cost per copy.

4. PERFORM research on independently published books that are similar to yours in terms of genre and page count. Don't expect to be able to compete with books published by major houses such as Simon & Schuster or HarperCollins. Their printing and shipping overhead will always be lower than yours because of the enormous volume of copies they print for each title.

5. ADD a profit margin, but make sure your book's pricing remains competitive with or even undercuts other books in its class.

Before choosing a low profit margin, consider whether you might wish to discount your copies for personal appearances. I subtract between two and five dollars from each book's cover price to give my booth's customers extra incentive to purchase my copies on the day of the event.

Whether you decide to include your book's price on its back cover depends upon whether you plan to change the price periodically or distribute it to bookstores, gift shops, and other brick-and-mortar markets. It's more helpful to retailers to provide the price printed on the cover, and it looks more professional since that's the industry standard practice.

A special note about hardcover dust jackets: Direct your cover designer to add the price to the inside front flap, which translates to the top right corner of the PDF image. If no price is present in that position, the bookseller could assume that the book was either independently published or that they have been given a book club edition. Neither assumption will help you sell copies to that retail outlet.

4N2. Setting the E-book's Price

E-BOOK PRICING is trickier than pricing print editions because with the establishment of a vendor account for digital publishing comes the relative ease of controlling your book's pricing.

When establishing the price of your book's digital edition, you need to ask yourself whether you would rather maximize the number of downloads or maximize your royalties.

The math for maximizing downloads is simple: the lower the price, the more downloads your book is likely to achieve.

Hang tight while I walk you through the weeds of maximizing your royalties.

The major e-book distribution platforms—including Nook Press, Kobo, and KDP—force authors to establish a minimum price of $2.99 in order to earn the company's highest royalty payout percentage. Furthermore, Nook Press and KDP force a $9.99 price cap. For books priced at $10.00 and higher, the author earns the same royalty payout rate as at the $0.99 tier.

Amazon is by far the largest—and stingiest—distributor, so I will use it in my royalty calculation examples here. For all Kindle e-books, the minimum price to earn 70 percent royalties is $2.99, and it must be priced no higher than $9.99; otherwise, the author earns only 35 percent.

If you wish to maximize your Amazon profits, then you need to price your e-book to fall within the 70 percent royalty window. At a 70 percent royalty rate, a $2.99 book will earn the author $2.09 per download. At $0.99

and an enforced royalty rate of 35 percent, your book will earn $0.35 per download. It will take six sales at $0.99 to surpass the royalties earned from one sale of a $2.99 book. If you think your title will perform well when priced at $2.99 or more, then go for it!

There exists a great temptation to set a price and leave it in perpetuity. That's the easiest approach, but unless you have decided to make your book permafree, in the long run that practice will cause more harm than good for its sales figures.

The preorder/launch price

THE LAUNCH price of an e-book depends upon a number of factors, including:

- **AN author's popularity.** The bigger your fan base, the more you can get away with pricing your books higher than their competitors.
- **WHETHER the book is fiction or nonfiction.** Like it or not, digital fiction is now being perceived almost as a commodity, with readers demanding to be able to read an author's blood, sweat, and tears for nothing or next to it. Not so with nonfiction e-books, which can attract a fair number of readers even when priced at $9.99 or more.
- **THE popularity of your book's genre or subject matter.** In general, books written for more popular genres can enjoy more sales at higher prices, but in a decision between two books by different authors, where both authors are unknown to the customer, she will usually opt for the lower-priced book unless influenced by other factors such as reviews, cover appeal, or synopsis.

- **IF part of a series, its sequence number.** Most authors discount or make permafree the first book in their series after other installments become available. This entices readers to acquire the earlier works for a modest investment, potentially earning the author more fans along the way.

If you're like most independent authors whose work struggles to bob above the ocean of books available to readers, then you may be better advised to launch your title at $0.99 and hope to attract proportionally more readers at the lower price point.

That's how I, as a relatively unknown author at the time, was able to get nearly two thousand paid downloads of my medieval paranormal romance *Snow in July* during the first three months following its July 2014 release with almost no advertising on my part. Those aren't astronomical numbers by any stretch of the imagination, but the performance was good enough to keep *Snow in July* lodged in Amazon's top twenty for the category of teen and young adult historical romance for several weeks running, earning many more downloads by readers who habitually shop off the first page of the category rankings.

The $0.99 book launch strategy is by no means a proven formula; so many other factors affect buying decisions, including a book's cover, genre, synopsis, keywords, and its author's popularity. But in today's climate of digital fiction being perceived as a commodity, it's not a bad plan to follow.

Regarding preorders

ONE WAY to generate buzz about your book's launch is

by establishing a preorder phase prior to its release. The only e-book vendor of note that does not permit preorders is Nook Press. You might be able to circumvent this limitation by releasing your title through a third-party distributor such as Draft2Digital or Smashwords, though I haven't yet tried this option. If you set up a Nook Press vendor account and stipulate a future publication date for your new e-book, you will have to return to your "Projects" page on or after the day in question to manually press the "Publish" button.

Caution: When defining a preorder period on Amazon, stick with the release date that you have chosen. If you change it, especially in regard to releasing the e-book earlier than planned, Amazon could penalize your vendor account by prohibiting any further books from being set up for preorder for the period of one year. This happened to me, and you will do well to learn from my mistake.

Amazon's Kindle Unlimited promotional tools

ONE ADVANTAGE to enrolling your book in Amazon's KDP Select program is access to Amazon's free marketing tools: the free promo days and the "countdown" deals.

A **free Kindle promo deal** is self-explanatory: You decide which days out of the ninety-day KDP Select enrollment period in which to offer your book free to all Amazon customers, regardless of whether or not they have purchased a Kindle Unlimited subscription. Amazon limits you to five free days out of every ninety that the title is enrolled in KDP Select, and you may decide whether and when to schedule these days. I have discovered the best results when I've scheduled my books' free deals to run on weekdays, and no more than two days in a row.

A **Kindle countdown deal** is a bit more involved, since you define not only the promotional period but the way in which the deal is offered to customers. For a book with a regular price of $3.99, for example, you might perhaps elect to offer it at $0.99 for the first two days, after which time the price automatically raises to $1.99, then $2.99. The idea is to provide a burst of sales at the lowest price, boosting the book's rank and thereby encouraging readers to still buy it at the higher pricing tiers.

I have yet to schedule any Kindle countdown deals but plan to try the service soon. I've heard of authors reaping far more success by scheduling a price of $0.99 for the duration of the countdown period rather than raising it incrementally until the full retail price is achieved.

Breathing new life into an older e-book release
THE SAME caution against setting an e-book's price in perpetuity applies to older titles, perhaps even more so, for several reasons.

1. LOWERING a book's price periodically is a good way to entice new readers to try your work. This technique is especially helpful if you run regular Amazon giveaways to build your audience there. Everyone who follows your Amazon author profile will receive an email notification whenever you have manually dropped the price on one of your titles, which can come in handy to give your featured book a ranking boost prior to its scheduled advertising promotion, such as a BookBub promotion. Success tends to breed success, and you cannot take advantage of this marketing principle if you never change your book's price.

2. AMAZON has begun changing their comparative pricing policy on all products. For books, this means that they will eventually stop comparing your title's print and Kindle edition pricing on the book's product page. In other words, once they have completed this policy switch, you will no longer see your book's print price crossed out, with its Kindle edition price underneath, to urge customers to buy the digital edition.

3. IF you don't drop your book's price at other retail sites such as Nook Press and Kobo, you won't be able to avail yourself of Amazon's price-matching feature. Seeing the regular digital price crossed out with the price-matched value in bold print underneath can be a powerful sales incentive for many customers, especially those who are already predisposed to purchase your work. Everyone likes to believe that they are getting a great deal, and this technique is an effective way to create that impression. Amazon will not, however, email your followers with news of price-matched discounts of your book.

4. EVEN setting a permanent $0.99 price for your book may hurt your sales in the long run. Unless you're planning to offer it free every six months, you won't be able to run a $0.99 promotion on BookBub due to their rule that a book will not be considered if it has been offered at the submitted deal price for more than fourteen days out of the past ninety.

If you're looking to do something drastic to breathe new life into an older title, especially if you have invested in a new cover and have overhauled the text, you cannot get more drastic than unpublishing it on all platforms and then relaunching it a few months later. I have seen some authors take this action, though I possess no insight regarding how their books' sales fared after relaunch.

The key takeaway is that you are given tremendous power with your vendor account to steer your book's retail career, and you will be well advised to take full advantage of this power everywhere you release your book for sale.

40. Digital Distribution Strategies for E-books, or "Bewitched, Bothered, and Bewildered by Amazon"

I F I HAD written this section before June of 2016, I would have begun with the advice to release a new e-book on Kindle Unlimited and keep it exclusively with Amazon for at least a year prior to releasing it on other platforms such as Nook Press and the iBooks Store.

Now I know better.

Before I launch into the horror stories, let me start with the basics.

Amazon, with its proprietary e-reader device, the Kindle, in all its sundry flavors, has become the largest distributor of e-books on the planet. Amazon also pays the lowest royalty rates to authors under most circumstances, a mere 35 percent, while forcing authors and publishers into a very narrow pricing window ($2.99–$9.99) in order to earn that coveted 70 percent royalty payout.

Oh, and by the way, if you have discounted your title to less than $2.99, that kicks you back into the 35 percent payout rate for the week, even on sales that were made at $2.99 prior to the price reduction.

Authors who have enrolled their titles in KDP Select (known as Kindle Unlimited to paying subscribers) have it even worse now that Amazon has gone to a per-page-read model for payments. As of this writing, the typical payout is about $0.004 (four-tenths of a penny) per reported page read. This means that an author needs to have a customer read at least 88 pages of an e-book priced at $0.99 in order to earn the same royalty amount (at the 35 percent payout rate) as a regular paid download.

What? You've published a novella on Kindle Unlimited that Amazon has deemed is less than 88 pages? Tough luck, my friend. Write something longer next time.

I won't comment upon the allegation raised by many author-bloggers that Amazon cannot accurately tell how much of a book has been read by a customer, but you are welcome to read the facts reported by *The Guardian* in "Authors Lose Out Again in Amazon Pay-per-page Scam" (https://www.theguardian.com/technology/2016/apr/26/authors-lose-out-again-in-amazon-pay-per-page-scam).

While there are short-term advantages to releasing a book to Kindle Unlimited, such as the ability to set up five free promotional days in every ninety-day enrollment period, in the long run you are not doing yourself or your book any favors by selling it on Amazon exclusively. Furthermore, you expose yourself to the risk of having your account shut down without warning (keep reading to get to those horror stories).

Before you panic, however, there are other distribution options to consider:

- **NOOK Press** (https://www.nookpress.com/). The royalty payout is 40 percent for books priced at less than $2.99 and more than $9.99. All other books earn a payout rate of 65 percent.
- **KOBO** (https://writinglife.kobobooks.com/). The royalty payout is 45 percent for books priced at $2.98 or less; otherwise, authors earn a 70 percent payout rate, even for titles priced higher than $9.99.

- **GOOGLE Play** (https://play.google.com/books/publish/). Per their overview, the author keeps "most" (in theory, more than 50 percent) of what is earned in download sales. I could not find any specific royalty payout schedule, and I have no sales data for this platform since I deactivated my books there in 2015, after a brief trial period. I did, however, find a royalty payout rate of 52 percent reported by third-party distributor Pronoun (see below).

- **IBOOKS Store** (http://www.apple.com/itunes/working-itunes/sell-content/books/book-faq.html). The vendor account for this retailer is easiest to manage if you have Apple equipment (i.e., a Mac or iPad). As with Google Play, I could not locate the royalty payout schedule, but according to Pronoun, it is 70 percent regardless of the book's price.

- **DRAFT2DIGITAL** (https://draft2digital.com/). This is my third-party distributor of choice for platforms such as the iBooks Store, Scribd, and others. The royalty payout is 60 percent for all books regardless of price, even to Nook and Kobo platforms.

- **SMASHWORDS** (https://www.smashwords.com/). The royalty payout varies by book's price and the origin of the sale, whether affiliate (see https://www.smashwords.com/about/supportfaq#Affiliate), nonaffiliate, or premium catalog (see https://www.smashwords.com/distribution) retailers. The premium catalog retailer category earns 60 percent payout regardless of the book's price. For a book priced at $0.99, the payout is 47–60 percent, with affiliate sales earning the lowest rate and premium catalog retail sales earning the highest. At $1.99, the payout rate is 58–70 percent, with the highest rate going to nonaffiliate rather than premium catalog retail sales. When the book's price is set at $2.99 or higher, the premium catalog retailer rate of 60 percent is the lowest tier, with nonaffiliate sales earning progressively higher royalty percentages of at least 74 percent.

- **PRONOUN** (https://pronoun.com/). In general, they follow the aforementioned retailers' royalty payment rates, with the notable exception of Nook, which they list as a flat rate of 50 percent rather than the price-dependent 40 percent or 65 percent. (Source: http://support.pronoun.com/knowledge_base/topics/what-are-the-retailers-distribution-fees) In addition, they offer distribution to Google Play, which could be advantageous since Google Play's title setup procedure is clunky and difficult to navigate. Just keep in mind that they tell you that you keep 100 percent of your *earnings* (i.e., the net after each retailer has taken its commission), not 100 percent of the list price.

In theory, you could use Smashwords to distribute your $0.99 e-book to Kindle, Nook, and Kobo and earn at least 47 percent royalties rather than Amazon's miserly 35 percent, Nook's 40 percent, or Kobo's 45 percent. Or you could use Draft2Digital as your distributor and get 60 percent royalties from Nook and Kobo (they do not support distribution to Kindle), or you could give Pronoun a try. I don't have direct experience with these strategies since I code my own e-books and have vendor accounts for all platforms except the iBooks Store, to whom I distribute using Draft2Digital.

There are other publishing platforms out there, such as StreetLib (https://www.streetlib.com/meetstreetlibus/), which takes a 10 percent commission on author sales over and above what the retail platforms collect. My advice is to read the fine print, and don't go with any outfit that tacks on its own fee on each sale. Once you have set up your book in their database, they are adding no further value for you, and they're using that sales commission to offset their own overhead costs.

Now, as promised, the horror stories about Amazon's Kindle Unlimited. I'll leave you to discover them for yourself:

- "THINK You Couldn't Possibly Lose Your Amazon Publishing Account? Think Again." An eye-opener about whether or not to permit Amazon exclusivity via Kindle Unlimited. (https://the-active-voice.com/2016/06/16/think-you-couldnt-possibly-lose-your-amazon-publishing-account-think-again/) by Becca Mills, 6/16/16, from *The Active Voice*. The author in question eventually got her KDP vendor account reinstated, but who needs that fresh hell from an employer who sits up nights trying to figure out new ways to withhold money from its legitimate content providers?
- "INNOCENT Authors Are Getting Burned in Amazon's Fight against KU Bot Farms" (http://the-digital-reader.com/2016/06/17/authors-are-getting-caught-up-in-amazons-fight-against-ku-bot-farms/) by Nate Hoffelder, 6/17/16, from *The Digital Reader*.
- "WHY I Refuse to Join Kindle Unlimited" (http://blather.michaelwlucas.com/archives/2703) by Michael Lucas, 6/17/16, from *Blather.MichaelWLucas*.

In short, Amazon is the big boy on the digital publishing block, knows it, and doesn't care how many innocent (or, as Michael Lucas put it, "low-value") authors they shaft with their automated fraud-detection schemes.

Are you frightened enough to pull out of KDP Select / Kindle Unlimited yet? You should be.

I have pulled all of my books except one out of automatic enrollment in Kindle Unlimited. The pittance I receive for participation in that marketing ploy is not worth the risk of having my account deactivated and my books delisted without warning due to fraudulent activity on someone else's part. The exception is my graphic novel, and at twenty-nine pages I would know that something fishy was going on if I saw a spike of hundreds of KU pages read on a single day.

Whether or not you set up multiple vendor or third-party accounts for distributing your books is of course up to you, but I will leave you with a parting point to ponder.

Since I have many titles in my personal catalog and many customers who read one of my books and then choose to purchase one or more of my other titles, I prefer to make that hunt easy by embedding product links in my "Other Books By" section of each e-book. You cannot do this as effectively if you publish via a middle-man like Pronoun. During the upload and verification process, Nook Press will reject any book that contains Amazon links, and so forth. So if you go with Pronoun, Draft2Digital, Smashwords, or another third party for distribution to the major retailers, you must upload a version that either contains no product links whatsoever or contains links to noncompeting sites such as eBay's Half.com, BooksAMillion, or the universal e-book links generated by Books2Read.

Even the practice of using universal book links

requires that I maintain retailer-specific versions of each title, which can be a pain when I've published a new book and then have to revisit all the other books to add its link for the appropriate retail platform. However, I've found the exercise to be well worthwhile, especially during a major marketing campaign such as a BookBub feature.

THE END... OR IS IT?

T HERE'S NO GREATER feeling in the world for a writer than reaching that blessed point in the project when one can type...

The End

Anyone who has ever completed the publication process, however, knows that "The End" signals the beginning of the rest of that manuscript's life as a published work.

There will be mistakes to correct, formatting updates to implement, perhaps even new text to add as you expand your catalog of published works and want to keep your readers informed of developments in your writing career.

How you react to these myriad decisions is up to you, of course. It is my fondest hope that I have armed you with enough information to make the best decisions possible for your unique circumstances.

Best of luck in all your writing, publishing, and marketing endeavors!

Kim Headlee
STORIES make us greater.
NOVEMBER 9, 2016
WYTHEVILLE, VA

P.S. IF you have liked this book—or even if you haven't—please consider leaving a review; thanks. And if you've loved it, please spread the word!

APPENDIX

Acronyms, Definitions, Organizations, and Other Critters

HERE BE DRAGONS. Or a collection of references; it's hard to tell which. They can look alike, though I'll inch out onto a limb to assert that the references might be safer to handle and more useful. For personal security reasons, please don't quote me on that.

Species such as the certified public accountant are so plentiful in the wild that I felt no need to clutter this list with their mention. I'll pay for that indiscretion later, I'm sure.

Book sections mentioning the dragon in question are noted in square brackets ("[]") at the end of its entry. When a dragon answers to more than one moniker, its most common appellation is listed first.

"#BookBub Promo Comparison: #Free vs. #99cents" (http://angelaroquet.blogspot.com/2016/08/bookbub-promo-comparison-free-vs-99cents.html). A blog post by author Angela Roquet. [4F3]

"10 Ways for Authors to Respond to Bad Reviews" (http://www.indieauthornews.com/2015/03/10-ways-for-authors-to-handle-bad-book-reviews.html). A blog post by Alan Kealey, news editor at *Indie Author News*. [4J2]

"11 BookBub Myths Busted" (http://insights.bookbub.com/bookbub-myths-busted/). A blog post by BookBub account coordinator Carlyn Robertson. [4F3]

24Symbols (https://www.24symbols.com/). An e-book and audiobook distributor mainly serving Europe. Authors may distribute their e-books to this service via Draft2Digital. Authors in a nonexclusive distribution agreement with ACX may in theory distribute their audiobook titles to 24Symbols, but you will have to contact them (info@24symbols.com) for more information about audiobook distribution. [4A4, 4G]

"5 Actions That Make Keywords Irrelevant" (http://www.sarkemedia.com/actions-that-make-keywords-irrelevant/). A blog post by entrepreneur Sarah Arrow. [4K2]

"5 Things Your Author Blog Should Have" (http://www.nikkiwoodsmedia.com/5-author-blog/). A blog post by author Nikki Woods. [4B2]

"5 Tips for Writing a Compelling Book Blurb" (http://romanceuniversity.org/2011/11/23/5-top-tips-for-writing-a-compelling-book-blurb-by-amy-wilkins/). A blog post about writing back-cover copy by by social media manager Amy Wilkins. [2D]

"5 Ways to Learn About Your Target Audience for Your Book" (http://e-booksindia.com/5-ways-to-learn-about-your-target-audience-for-your-book/).   A blog post by author Georgina Roy. [4K2]

"7 Tips to Write SEO Friendly Blog Posts" (http://www.iftiseo.com/2015/12/7-tips-to-write-seo-friendly-blog-posts.html). A blog post by content marketing specialist Julie Petersen. [4C]

"8 Tips for Getting Tons of Traffic to Your Blog and Making Lots of Money With It – and Why I'm Not Following Them" (http://www.lilistravelplans.com/8-tips-for-getting-tons-of-traffic-to-your-blog-and-making-lots-of-money-with-it-and-why-im-not-following-them/). A blog post about content writing techniques by travel blogger Liesbeth. [4B2]

"98 Book Marketing Tips" (http://insights.book-bub.com/book-marketing-ideas/).   A resource for all authors written by BookBub's Industry Marketing Manager, Diana Urban. [2D]

"A DIY Facebook Party in 7 Steps" (https://kimi-versonheadlee.blogspot.com/2015/09/the-business-of-writing-diy-facebook.html). A blog post written by *The Maze of Twisty Passages* contributor and author K.R. Thompson. [4A4]

ACX, a.k.a. Audiobook Creation eXchange (http://www.acx.com/). Amazon's business unit devoted to the production of audiobooks. [2G., 2G1, 2G2]

ACX cover requirements (http://audible-acx.custhelp.com/app/answers/detail/a_id/6654/kw/cover). A resource for graphic designers looking to create an audiobook cover suitable for ACX upload. [2E4]

Adobe InDesign. Document-layout software that may be used for producing fliers, banners, cards, and other promotional materials in addition to books. If you want to acquire this software, do an Internet search for "**Adobe InDesign CS6**"—the final version available for installation on your computer. It's vanishingly rare, though; eBay may be your best bet since InDesign CS6 is listed as "currently unavailable" on Amazon because Adobe (following Microsoft's lead) is pushing its users into the cloud-based computing versions. Cloud-based computing, in addition to being hideously expensive for the end user, is also hideously slow. For the health of your documents, your pocketbook, and your sanity, do not drink the cloud-based computing Kool-Aid offered by anyone. Adobe appends the acronym CC (Creative Cloud) to all its cloud-based computing software products. Its acronym CS (Creative Suite; e.g., InDesign CS6) applies to its "legacy" (i.e., local computer installable) software versions. [2F, 2F2]

    "**Advanced Applications of the Amazon Kindle Book Previewer**" (https://kimiversonheadlee.blogspot.com/2016/05/the-business-of-writing-advanced.html). Further waxing technical about the Kindle book previewer software by Kim Iverson Headlee. [4D]

    Amazon giveaway dashboard (https://www.amazon.com/giveaway/host/dashboard). When you are signed on to your Amazon account, this page displays information about your open and completed Amazon giveaways. [4E, 4H]

    ARC, a.k.a. advance reader copy. Any version, printed or digital, of your book that is distributed in advance of its publication date, usually for the purpose of soliciting reviews and creating publicity prior to the book's launch. [2F2, 4A1]

ASIN, a.k.a. Amazon Standard Identification Number. The ten-digit alphanumeric designation assigned by Amazon to a product listed in its catalog. For a print book, its ASIN is the same value as its ten-digit ISBN. [2A1, 4D, 4L3]

Aspect ratio. For images (e.g., book covers), this is a numerical value or expression that describes the proportional relationship between the image's width and height. A book cover that is 1600 x 2400 pixels has a numerical aspect ratio of 1.5, which is equivalent to the expression 3:2. A square format audiobook cover image (2400 x 2400 pixels) has an aspect ratio of 1.0 or 1:1. [2E1, 2F1]

Audiobook Fans (http://www.audiobookfans.com/review-policy/). A website for obtaining audiobook reviews. [2G3]

Audiobook Jukebox (http://audiobookjukebox.squarespace.com/solid-gold-reviewer-program/). A website for obtaining audiobook reviews that does not entail your having to part with your Audible free-download codes. [2G3]

Audiobook Review (http://audiobookreviewer.com/review-policy/). A website for obtaining audiobook reviews of science fiction and fantasy titles. [2G3]

Author Marketing Experts (http://www.amarketingexpert.com/). A company specializing in book marketing for authors. [4E]

Authors Guild, The (https://www.authorsguild.org/). America's oldest and largest professional organization for writers. [1B]

"Authors Lose Out Again in Amazon Pay-per-page Scam" (https://www.theguardian.com/technology/2016/apr/26/authors-lose-out-again-in-amazon-pay-per-page-scam). An article by *Guardian* technology reporter Alex Hern. [4O].

Awesome Gang (http://awesomegang.com/submit-your-book/). A free book-marketing service consisting of either email, website, or other social media promotion, or some combination thereof. Paid marketing options for guaranteed advertising placement may also be available. [4F1]

Back-cover copy. This is a publishing term referring to a book's short synopsis, so named because it most often appears on the back cover of the book's print edition. [2D]

BAM! Publish (http://www.bampublish.com/pricing). The division of Books-A-Million for book publishing and distribution. [2F]

Betty BookFreak (http://bettybookfreak.com/authors/). A paid book-marketing service consisting of either email, website, or other social media promotion, or some combination thereof. Free promotion opportunities may be available too. [4F2]

Bigstock by Shutterstock (http://www.bigstockphoto.com/). A website for obtaining licenses for stock photos, clipart, and videos. [2E1]

BISAC fiction codes (http://bisg.org/page/Fiction). The subsection of the BISAC subject headings list devoted to fiction. [4K1]

BISAC subject codes, a.k.a. BISAC subject headings (http://bisg.org/page/BISAC2015Edition). A list of several hundred book classification codes by subject matter maintained by the Subject Codes Committee of BISG. [4K1]

Bitly (https://bitly.com/). A link-shortening tool. The free service level offers five hundred branded bitlinks and five thousand total bitlinks. [4L3]

Bleed. In book-layout terminology, this refers to the practice of allowing background images and other artwork to extend beyond the edge of the page before it is trimmed. In other words, the bleed is the area that is cut off. [4N1]

Block, Julian (https://julianblocktaxexpert.com/). Tax attorney and author of *Julian Block's Easy Tax Guide For Writers, Photographers, And Other Freelancers*. [1C]

Blog tour, a.k.a. virtual book tour. An online social event that functions like a physical book tour by spreading the word about one or more of an author's books across the blogosphere. As with physical book tours, blog tours may be either DIY or professionally coordinated. [1B, 1E1, 1E2, 4A4, 4B2, 4H, 4I, 4J4]

Blogosphere. Yes, this is a bona fide word now. It's the official designation per the 16th edition of *Merriam-Webster's Collegiate Dictionary* referring to the cyberkingdom of blogs. [Preface, 4A11]

Book Barbarian (http://bookbarbarian.com/ad-requirements/). A paid book-marketing service consisting of either email, website, or other social media promotion, or some combination thereof. Free promotion opportunities may be available too. [4F2]

Book Industry Study Group Inc., a.k.a. BISG (http://bisg.org/). A US trade association for policy, technical standards, and research related to books and similar products. Its stated goal is "to create a more informed, empowered and efficient book community," which it does through maintenance of the BISAC subject codes and other industry advances. [4K1]

"Book Marketing: How and Why to Make a Self-published Book Permafree" (http://selfpublishingadvice.org/book-marketing-how-and-why-to-make-a-selfpublished-book-permafree/). A blog post by marketing expert Clare Flynn. [4G]

"Book Promotions ~ Indie Authors Report Results" (http://jackieweger.com/book-promotions-in-die-authors-report-results/). A blog post detailing the success of a BookBub promotion for a free book written by Scottish author Mary Smith. [4F3]

BookBub (https://www.bookbub.com/partners/pricing). E-book discovery service that boasts subscriber lists for various genres numbering at least in the hundreds of thousands. Subscriber lists for the most popular genres number in the millions. BookBub's recommendations for industry news sources, industry blogs, cover designers, book distributors and publishing services, book development and editing services, website building tools, and writers' communities are listed on this page: https://insights.bookbub.com/bookbub-favorite-publishing-resources/. [2D, 2E1, 4E, 4F3, 4N2, 4O]

BookBub deal checklist (https://www.bookbub.com/partners/checklist). A resource for BookBub advertising partners to ensure maximum success of the scheduled promotion. Or just bookmark this section in *The Business of Writing*: [4F3]

"BookBub Featured Deals vs. BookBub Ads: What's the Difference?" (https://insights.bookbub.com/bookbub-featured-deals-vs-bookbub-ads-whats-the-difference/). A blog post and infographic by BookBub Industry Marketing Manager Diana Urban. [4F3]

BookBub policies page (https://www.bookbub.com/partners/policies). A resource detailing an advertiser's responsibilities in relation to running a featured deal with BookBub. [4F3]

BookGorilla (http://www.bookgorilla.com/advertise). A paid book-marketing service consisting of either email, website, or other social media promotion, or some combination thereof. Free promotion opportunities may be available too. [4F2]

BookLife (http://booklife.com/). The website run by *Publishers Weekly* serving the needs of independent authors. Through this venue authors may request reviews, post news articles about their books, and participate in the annual contest sponsored by *BookLife*. [2G2, 4A1]

BookLinker (http://booklinker.net/). A website for establishing a single link for any product in the Amazon retail catalog that automatically redirects the page's visitor to the Amazon business unit operating in or closest to the visitor's country. The BookLinker service is free as of this writing. [4A4, 4L2, 4M2]

Books Butterfly (http://www.booksbutterfly.com/). A paid book-marketing service consisting of either email, website, or other social media promotion, or some combination thereof. Free promotion opportunities may be available too. [4F2]

Books for Ears (http://booksforears.com/contact-us/). A website for obtaining audiobook reviews. [2G3]

Books on the Knob (https://docs.google.com/forms/d/1DlL2gaFaDtcTbjZSTE-zsGD4HOvHRccShMyy-cCgqfGs/viewform). A free book-marketing service consisting of either email, website, or other social media promotion, or some combination thereof. Paid marketing options for guaranteed advertising placement may also be available. [4F1]

Books2Read   (https://books2read.com/faq/author/). A website for establishing a single link to all known retail sites for an e-book. [4A4, 4L2, 4O]

BookSends (http://booksends.com/advertise.php). A paid book-marketing service consisting of either email, website, or other social media promotion, or some combination thereof. Free promotion opportunities may be available too. [4F2]

Booktrack (https://promo.booktrack.com/self-publish). An audiobook production service that's priced competitively with ACX. [2G2]

Bookworms and Writers (http://www.bookwormsandwriters.com/). A free book-marketing service consisting of either email, website, or other social media promotion, or some combination thereof. Paid marketing options for guaranteed advertising placement may also be available. [4F1]

Bookzio   (http://www.bookzio.com/submit-a-listing/). A free book-marketing service consisting of either email, website, or other social media promotion, or some combination thereof. Paid marketing options for guaranteed advertising placement may also be available. [4F1]

Bowker (https://www.myidentifiers.com), a.k.a. R. R. Bowker LLC. Currently owned by Cambridge Information Group, this company is the exclusive US agent for assigning ISBNs. Its history of supporting the publishing industry dates back to the 1860s and is linked to the founding of the publishing trade magazine *Publishers Weekly*. In addition to ISBN assignment, Bowker manages the definitive database of publisher imprints and releases the annual *Books in Print* bibliographic compilation of published works. [2A1, 2A2, 4K1]

Calibre (http://calibre-ebook.com/). Free library-management software that can be used for creating EPUB, MOBI, and other digital file types from native HTML and other source formats. [2F1]

CD Baby (http://members.cdbaby.com/faq.aspx). An audiobook distributor open to authors in a nonexclusive distribution agreement with ACX. [2G1]

Circle Legal (http://www.circlelegal.com/). An American law firm. I have no affiliation with this company. [1C]

Claim. There exist two definitions for the purposes of this book:

1. THE function exercised using the eCO platform whereby an author or publisher initiates the copyright registration process for a book. [1F2]
2. THE function exercised using the ACX platform whereby an author, publisher, or other type of rights holder begins the audiobook production process by associating a book in Amazon's product catalog with the rights holder's ACX account. [2G1]

Copyright Law of the United States (http://www.copyright.gov/title17/), a.k.a. Title 17. The complete contents of Title 17, which governs the application of US copyright law. [1F2]

Copyright Office Fees*, a.k.a. *Circular 4 (http://www.copyright.gov/fls/sl04.pdf). A resource for US copyright claimants detailing the fees for registering a copyright under various circumstances. [1F2]

Cover reveal. A specialized form of blog tour designed to build excitement (or "buzz," in industry parlance) about a book by unveiling its cover, which is usually available several weeks or months before the book goes on sale. [1E1, 4A4]

CreateSpace (https://www.createspace.com). Amazon's original platform for publishing paperback books. [1A, 2A1, 2E3, 2F, 2F2, 4A1, 4H, 4K2, 4N1]

Crowdfire (http://crowdfireapp.com/). A Twitter account management service that allows the user to quickly check nonfollowers, recent followers, recent unfollowers, and so forth. Crowdfire offers free as well as paid service options. [4A12, 4L2]

CSS, a.k.a. cascading style sheets. A language used for describing the presentation of a document written in any markup language, most commonly HTML and XHTML. [2F1]

Dawnflier, The (http://eepurl.com/boiQ0z). The monthly newsletter of Kim Iverson Headlee that offers gifts, exclusive giveaway links, advance notice of BookBub promotions, upcoming personal appearances, and other news to subscribers. [4A11, 4E]

Depositphotos (http://depositphotos.com/). A website for obtaining licenses for stock photos, clipart, and videos. [2E1]

Digital Book Today (http://digitalbooktoday.com/join-our-team/paid-and-free-promotions/). A paid book-marketing service consisting of either email, website, or other social media promotion, or some combination thereof. Free promotion opportunities may be available too. [4F2]

Discount Book Man (http://discountbookman.com/book-promotion/). A free book-marketing service consisting of either email, website, or other social media promotion, or some combination thereof. Paid marketing options for guaranteed advertising placement may also be available. [4F1]

DiscountMugs   (https://www.discountmugs.com). A website for purchasing branded marketing materials. [4M3]

"DIY Blog Tours" (https://kimiversonheadlee.blog-spot.com/2015/10/the-business-of-writing-diy-blog-tours.html). A blog post written by *The Maze of Twisty Passages* contributor Liza O'Connor. [4A4]

"DIY Book Trailers, Part 1: Do Your Homework!" (http://kimiversonheadlee.blogspot.com/2015/09/the-business-of-writing-do-your.html). Reblogged on *The Maze* with permission of author Nancy Cohen. [4A8]

"DIY Book Trailers, Part 2: Now What?" (http://kimiversonheadlee.blogspot.com/2015/09/the-business-of-writing-now-what-diy.html). Reblogged on *The Maze* with permission of author Nancy Cohen. [4A8]

DM, a.k.a. direct message. A private message sent from one Twitter user to another. A DM may be sent only to a user who follows you. If it transpires that I follow your Twitter account, I welcome your personal questions and comments, but please do not send me automated DMs. Ever. Thank you. [4L1, 4L2]

"Do I or Don't I?" (http://beverleybateman.blogspot.com/2015/10/do-i-or-dont-i.html). A blog post about whether to publish an author newsletter by Beverly Bateman. [4E]

"Do You Have a Hobby or Business?" (http://she-ownsit.com/do-you-have-a-hobby-or-business/). A blog post by Kelly Keller, president of Circle Legal law firm. [1C]

Draft2Digital   (https://www.draft2digital.com/). Third-party distributor of e-book content to major e-tailer sites such as Nook Press and Kobo. [1D, 1E1, 2A1, 4A4, 4F3, 4G, 4K1, 4N2, 4O]

Dreamstime (https://www.dreamstime.com/). A website for obtaining licenses for stock photos, clipart, and videos. [2E1]

eBook Soda (http://www.ebooksoda.com/authors/). A paid book-marketing service consisting of either email, website, or other social media promotion, or some combination thereof. Free promotion opportunities may be available too. [4F2]

eBookasaurus (http://ebookasaurus.com/free-book-listing/). A free book-marketing service consisting of either email, website, or other social media promotion, or some combination thereof. Paid marketing options for guaranteed advertising placement may also be available. [4F1]

eBooks Habit (http://ebookshabit.com/for-authors/). A free book-marketing service consisting of either email, website, or other social media promotion, or some combination thereof. Paid marketing options for guaranteed advertising placement may also be available. [4F1]

eCO, a.k.a. Electronic Copyright Office (http://www.copyright.gov/eco/). The website run by the Library of Congress for registering the US copyright of a book or other type of physical or digital content. [1F2]

Editorial license. A type of license for photos, illustrations, videos, and other media; it restricts the user to noncommercial applications. [2E1]

EPUB. A rigidly structured ZIP file containing all elements of an e-book, coded in HTML, that are required for display on almost all types of e-reader devices except Kindles. [2F1, 4G]

EPUBCheck (http://validator.idpf.org/). A free EPUB online validation software tool created by the

International Digital Publishing Forum. Individuals who don't need to run EPUBCheck on large numbers of files may use the online version; e-book distribution plat-forms and large publishers are required to install the app. [2F1, 4G]

eReader Girl (http://ereadergirl.com/sub-mit-your-ebook/). A free book-marketing service con-sisting of either email, website, or other social media promotion, or some combination thereof. Paid marketing options for guaranteed advertising placement may also be available. [4F1]

Ereader News Today (http://ereadernewstoday.com/pricing/), a.k.a. ENT. A paid book-marketing service consisting of either email, website, or other social media promotion, or some combination thereof. Free promo-tion opportunities may be available too. [4F2, 4F3]

Every Writer Resource (http://everywritersre-source.com/selfpublished/submit-your-book/). A free book-marketing service consisting of either email, web-site, or other social media promotion, or some combi-nation thereof. Paid marketing options for guaranteed advertising placement may also be available. [4F1]

Eye on Romance (http://www.eyeonromance.com/forauthors.cfm). A paid book-marketing service consist-ing of either email, website, or other social media pro-motion, or some combination thereof. Free promotion opportunities may be available too. [4F2]

Feed140 (https://feed140.net/home). A Twitter content management service. Caution: Do not create an account with Feed140 unless you're serious about using this service. They will annoy you to the boiling point with their barrage of emails. When they were pestering me, there was no way to unsubscribe so I had to report them as spam (which in fact those emails were, since they didn't offer an unsubscribe option) to get them to quit. [4A11]

Form TX (http://www.copyright.gov/forms/formtx.pdf). The US Copyright Office application and instructions for initiating the paper process of registering the copyright of a book rather than utilizing the Electronic Copyright Office website. The most important thing the form's instructions doesn't mention is the processing fee, which as of this writing is $85.00. [1F2]

Fostering Success (http://www.fostering-success.com/). The author services company of *New York Times* and *USA Today* best-selling romance author Melissa Foster. Her associate for graphic design, Natasha Brown, is the primary book cover artist (http://www.fostering-success.com/author-services-book-covers-formatting-marketing/ebook-cover-design) employed by Kim Iverson Headlee, and she is listed as one of BookBub's favorite cover designers. [2E1]

Free Book Dude (http://www.freebookdude.com/2016/05/advertising-and-promotion-options-with.html). A free book-marketing service consisting of either email, website, or other social media promotion, or some combination thereof. Paid marketing options for guaranteed advertising placement may also be available. [4F1]

Free99Books (http://free99books.com/author/add). A free book-marketing service consisting of either email, website, or other social media promotion, or some combination thereof. Paid marketing options for guaranteed advertising placement may also be available. [4F1]

Frugal Freebies (http://www.frugal-freebies.com/p/submit-freebie.html). A free book-marketing service consisting of either email, website, or other social media promotion, or some combination thereof. Paid marketing options for guaranteed advertising placement may also be available. [4F1]

Fussy Librarian, The (http://www.thefussylibrar-ian.com/for-authors/). A paid book-marketing service consisting of either email, website, or other social media promotion, or some combination thereof. Free promotion opportunities may be available too. [4F2]

Genre Pulse (http://www.genrepulse.com/how-it-works/). A paid book-marketing service consisting of either email, website, or other social media promotion, or some combination thereof. Free promotion opportunities may be available too. [4F2]

"Get Clear on You" (http://sheownsit.com/30912-2/). A blog post about personal branding for entrepreneurs by *She Owns It* featured contributor Lorea M. Sample. [3A]

GIFCreator (http://gifcreator.me/). A free tool that allows the creation of animated memes using your own photos and other images. What separates this software from the pack is that they do not embed advertising watermarks in your GIF files as other "free" online tools are wont to do. Please make sure you have read the section in this book about the use of images you don't own before you dash off a jillion memes. The GIFCreator website also offers the ability to resize and compress GIFs, perform PDF to JPG conversion, and manage passwords. [3A]

GoDaddy (http://www.godaddy.com). A domain procurement and website management service. [4E]

Goddess Fish (http://www.goddessfish.com/services/). An author services provider used by Kim Iverson

Headlee. [4A4]

Goodreads (https://www.goodreads.com/). A book-discussion forum owned and operated by Amazon, although to their credit they have left it pretty much alone since acquiring it from its founders in 2013, aside from moving Shelfari users and content to the Goodreads platform in 2016 prior to closing Shelfari. Visitors to Shelfari.com are now redirected to Goodreads and shown a merger message. [4H]

Goodreads Author Program (https://www.goodreads.com/author/program). Open to all writers, even those who have not yet published a book. [4H]

Goodreads Librarians Group (https://www.goodreads.com/group/show/220-goodreads-librarians-group). A Goodreads forum wherein authors or their authorized representatives may interact with super librarians to seek information and solve book database issues that the author cannot address using options available via his or her own Goodreads account. [3B]

Google Play (https://play.google.com/books/publish/). The digital content (including e-books) distribution service managed by Google. [1E1, 2A1, 2G2, 4A4, 4F3, 4O]

Great Books Great Deals (https://greatbooksgreatdeals.wufoo.com/forms/gbgd-authors/). A free book-marketing service consisting of either email, website, or other social media promotion, or some combination thereof. Paid marketing options for guaranteed advertising placement may also be available. [4F1]

Griffin Editorial Services (http://griffineditorial.com/). Owned and operated by Robin Allen, this is another editorial services company employed by Kim Iverson Headlee. [2B]

Gutter, a.k.a. inside margin. A publishing term representing the page margins closest to the book's spine. [2F2]

Half.com (http://www.half.ebay.com/). The website maintained by eBay for fixed-price listings of books, textbooks, music, movies, and games. Vendors do not pay upfront listing fees, all entries stay in the catalog until sold, vendors are partially reimbursed for shipping costs, and Half.com makes a modest commission on each sale. Buyers share their payment information only with Half.com, never with the seller. I've found the site useful for advertising autographed copies of my books at my in-person prices, but items must exist in Half.com's catalog. Typically it takes about six months for a new book to be picked up by Half.com. [4O]

Hashtag. A collection of alphanumeric characters hyperlinked to searches on sites such as Twitter, Facebook, and other social media. These character groupings (or tags) are preceded by the symbol #, also called a hashmark; hence the term hashtag. [4C, 4L1]

Hootsuite (http://hootsuite.com/). As of this writing, this is the most widely used social media management tool in the world... and the most stable in terms of Twitter not shutting it down since its 2009 inception. [4A11, 4L3]

Hot Damn Stock (http://hotdamnstock.com/). A website for obtaining licenses for stock photos. [2E1]

"How 140 Characters Can Stand Out on Twitter" (http://blog.socedo.com/how-140-characters-can-stand-out-on-twitter/). A blog post by Teena Thach. [4L3]

"How Authors Can Become Better Bloggers" (http://e-booksindia.com/how-authors-can-become-better-bloggers/). A blog post by freelance content writer Kavitha. [4B2]

"How BookBub's Selection Process Works" (https://insights.bookbub.com/how-bookbub-selection-process-works/). A resource for authors, publishers, and publicists considering the possibility of scheduling a BookBub featured deal campaign. [4F3]

"How to Create an Interior PDF of Your Book" (https://www.createspace.com/Products/Book/InteriorPDF.jsp). A CreateSpace resource that provides information for basic book layout design, including the establishment of inside (gutter) and outside margins. [2F2].

"How to Use Goodreads to Dramatically Grow Your Audience" (http://mixtusmedia.com/blog/how-to-use-goodreads-to-dramatically-grow-your-audience). A blog post by Jenn Hanson-dePaula. [4H]

"How to Use SEO for Authors" (http://mfrw.blogspot.com/2015/12/how-to-use-seo.html). A blog post by MFRW founder Kayelle Allen. [4C]

"How to Use Song Lyrics in Your Book" (http://www.betternovelproject.com/blog/song-lyrics/). A blog post by attorney Kathryn Goldman. [2C]

"How Your Newsletter Can Get You More Readers, Visibility, and Sales" (http://www.amarketingexpert.com/how-your-newsletter-can-get-you-more-readers-visibility-and-sales/). A blog post about increasing the effectiveness of your author newsletter. [4E]

HTML Dog (http://www.htmldog.com/). A comprehensive online reference for HTML tags and CSS programming information. [2F1]

iBooks Store, The (http://www.apple.com/itunes/working-itunes/sell-content/books/book-faq.html). The platform for publishing books formatted for display on Apple's phones, computers, and tablets. [1E1, 4A4, 4F3, 4G, 4O]

Illustrated Romance, The (https://illustratedromance.com/). A website for obtaining licenses for stock photos. [2E1]

Imprint. In publishing, this is a label that defines a body of work (e.g., Pocket Books). [1A, 1E1, 2A2, 2B, 2D, 2E1, 4M2]

Indie Book of the Day (http://indiebookoftheday.com/authors/free-on-kindle-listing/). A free book-marketing service consisting of either email, website, or other social media promotion, or some combination thereof. Paid marketing options for guaranteed advertising placement may also be available. [4F1]

Indie Reviewers List (http://www.theindieview.com/indie-reviewers/). A long list, maintained by *The Indie View*, of bloggers willing to review independently published books. [4J4]

IngramSpark (http://www.ingramspark.com/). The business unit operated by Ingram Content Group, subsidiary of Ingram Industries, for serving the electronic and print-on-demand publishing needs of independent author-publishers. Royalty payments, service transactions such as title setup and revision fees, and order invoicing are handled by Lightning Source. [1A, 2E3, 2F2]

Inktera (http://www.inktera.com/store/). The e-book distribution platform formerly known as Page Foundry. [4G]

"Innocent Authors Are Getting Burned in Amazon's Fight against KU Bot Farms" (http://the-digital-reader.com/2016/06/17/authors-are-getting-caught-up-in-amazons-fight-against-ku-bot-farms/). A blog post by

Nate Hoffelder. [4O]

Interior Reviewer (https://www.createspace.com/Tools/InteriorReviewer.jsp). Launch page for CreateSpace's Interior Reviewer tool, which also provides a Word-to-PDF and RTF-to-PDF conversion option for print books. [2F2]

"IRS Standard Mileage Rates at a Glance" (http://www.irs.gov/Credits-&-Deductions/Individuals/Standard-Mileage-Rates-Glance). A US taxpayer reference detailing the allowed automobile mileage deduction rates for the current tax year. [1B]

ISBN (https://www.myidentifiers.com/help/isbn). The acronym for International Standard Book Number, a unique commercial book identifier that is thirteen digits for all ISBNs assigned on or after January 1, 2007. [2A1, 4H]

iStock by Getty Images (http://www.istockphoto.com/). A website for obtaining licenses for stock photos, clipart, and videos. [2E1]

"It Isn't Amazon Publishers Should Fear. It's BookBub." (http://www.huffingtonpost.com/mike-alvear/it-isnt-amazon-publishers_b_8307708.html). A blog post by nonfiction author Mike Alvear. [4F3]

It's Write Now (http://itswritenow.com/submit-your-book/). A free book-marketing service consisting of either email, website, or other social media promotion, or some combination thereof. Paid marketing options for guaranteed advertising placement may also be available. [4F1]

Julian Block's Easy Tax Guide For Writers, Photographers, And Other Freelancers (https://julian-blocktaxexpert.com/books/tax-tips-for-small-busi-nesses/). The paperback may be ordered from author

Julian Block. If you own a Kindle Unlimited subscription, you may download the 2014 e-book edition free (search on ASIN B00IKZ8C2U). Check Amazon for current non-KU pricing. [1C]

KDP, a.k.a. Kindle Direct Publishing (https://kdp.amazon.com/). Amazon's platform for publishing books formatted for display on Kindle devices. [1A, 1C, 1E1, 2A1, 2F1, 3A, 3B, 4F3, 4G, 4H, 4K2, 4N2]

KDP Print (https://kdp.amazon.com/help?topicId=A1MMZZIUU7LTIB). Amazon's newest platform for publishing a paperback book, the layout of which is based upon the book's Kindle edition. [2A1, 2E3, 4H, 4K1]

KDP Select (https://kdp.amazon.com/select?ref_=kdp_REP_TN_se). Amazon's e-book publishing option that requires 100 percent exclusivity in order for a title to remain eligible for enrollment. The referenced page blows a lot of smoke about its benefits to authors, but as with real smoke, it can be toxic when inhaled. To quote from section 5 (titled "Your Commitment") of Amazon's terms and conditions (https://kdp.amazon.com/help?topicId=APILE934L348N#Select) for KDP Select enrollment:

> If you don't comply with these KDP Select terms and conditions, we will not owe you Royalties for that Digital Book for the Kindle Subscription Programs or Kindle Owners' Lending Library Programs, and we may offset any of those Royalties that were previously paid against future Royalties, or require you to remit them to us. We may also withhold your Royalty payments on all your Digital Books for a period of up to 90 days while we investigate. **This doesn't limit other remedies we have,**

such as prohibiting your future participation in KDP Select or KDP generally. (emphasis mine)

In other words, do not incur the wrath of Amazon. [4F3, 4N2, 4O]

KDROI, a.k.a. Kindle Direct Return on Investment (http://www.5minutepublishing.com/dashboard/kdroi/). A browser plugin sold by 5MinutePublishing that allows the user to schedule unlimited promotions of free, permafree, and $0.99 Kindle e-books for a onetime fee. [4F1, 4F3]

Keyword. A significant word used in indexing or cataloging, or in labeling other text. [2D, 2F1, 4C, 4K2, 4N2]

Keyword density checker (http://smallseotools.com/keyword-density-checker/). A statistics tool to assist in search engine optimization for blog posts. [4C]

Kindle Book Previewer (http://www.amazon.com/b?ie=UTF8&node=13489836011). A book promotion tool offered by Amazon that allows an e-book's cover, interior preview, buy, and share functions to be embedded on a website via hyperlink or <iframe> HTML code. [4D]

Kindle Book Promos (http://kindlebookpromos.luckycinda.com/?page_id=283). A free book-marketing service consisting of either email, website, or other social media promotion, or some combination thereof. Paid marketing options for guaranteed advertising placement may also be available. [4F1]

Kindle Countdown Deal (https://kdp.amazon.com/help?topicId=A3288N75MH14B8). A book promotion service offered by KDP to e-books enrolled in KDP Select. [1E1, 4A4, 4N2]

Kindle Free Book Promotion (https://kdp.amazon.com/help?topicId=A34IQ0W14ZKXM9). A book promotion service offered by KDP to e-books enrolled in KDP Select. [1E1, 4A4, 4N2]

Kindle Unlimited, a.k.a. KU. Amazon's subscription service that allows unlimited access to e-books enrolled in KDP Select for one monthly fee. [1C, 1E1, 4F3, 4G, 4N2, 4O]

Kobo (https://writinglife.kobobooks.com/). The platform operated by Toronto-based Rakuten Kobo Inc. for publishing e-books formatted for display on Kobo e-readers. [1A, 1D, 1E1, 2A1, 4F3, 4G, 4K1, 4L2, 4N2, 4O]

Label. In the context of writing blog posts, the label functions as a specialized keyword that gets compiled into a searchable collection of commonly used terms within the blog. [4C]

LegalZoom (https://www.legalzoom.com/). A website for conducting legal affairs such as establishing a corporation. My son has used this site for setting up his corporation, but I have no experience with it. [1A]

LibraryThing (https://www.librarything.com/). An independent book-discussion forum for readers and authors. I pray to All That Is Holy that it will remain independent and not be gobbled up by Amazon as Goodreads was. [4H]

LibraryThing Authors (http://www.librarything.com/about/authors). A resource for programs available to authors and information regarding how to become a recognized author in LibraryThing. [4H]

LibraryThing Member Giveaways (http://www.librarything.com/wiki/index.php/HelpThing:Er list#How_do_I_give_away_books_with_the_Member_Giveaways_program.3F). A resource for learning how to set up giveaways through LibraryThing. [4H]

Lightning Source (http://www.ingramcontent. com/publishers/lp/lightning-source). The business unit operated by Ingram Content Group, subsidiary of Ingram Industries, serving the publishing needs of small presses as well as larger operations; prior to the formation of IngramSpark, independent authors also were permitted to establish accounts with Lightning Source. [4H]

Limited liability corporation. A type of corporate structure for small businesses. For a precise definition, please consult your lawyer or an online service such as LegalZoom. [1A]

Lucky Bat Books (http://www.luckybatbooks. com/). An author services company run by Judith Harlan, and Kim Iverson Headlee's primary provider of book interior layouts when she is not doing it herself. [2E1, 2F, 2F2]

Magic of Books Promotions (http://magicofbook-spromo.blogspot.com/p/welcome-to-magic-of-books-promotions.html). An author promotional services provider used by Kim Iverson Headlee. [4A4]

MailChimp (http://www.mailchimp.com). An email campaign and subscriber management service. The free version is sufficient for the needs of most independent authors. [4E]

"Make Your Book More Discoverable with Keywords" (https://kdp.amazon.com/help?topi-cId=A2EZES9JAJ6H02). An Amazon reference that provides best-practices advice for selecting a book's keywords. [4K2]

Marketing for Romance Writers, a.k.a. MFRW (http://marketingforromancewriters.org/). A free, peer-oriented mentoring group founded by author

Kayelle Allen that is now open to the entire literary community; Twitter handle @MFRW_ORG, primary hashtag #MRFWOrg. [4B, 4C]

Mass-market paperback. A small, inexpensive bookbinding format using low-quality paper that tends to discolor and disintegrate after a number of decades. The format is so named because typical print runs number in the tens of thousands—hence the need for the low-cost production method. [2D, 2G]

Maze of Twisty Passages, The, a.k.a. **The Maze** (http://kimiversonheadlee.blogspot.com). The blog of author Kim Iverson Headlee. Currently on Twitter's blacklist as a "potentially spam or malicious" website. It is neither, as you can see when you visit it. No ads, no morally offensive content, nothing, zilch, zip, nada—other than my supporting of other authors, posts about my own books and other news, my *Business of Writing* posts, and excerpts of my latest work in progress. None of the mirror sites (http://kimiversonheadlee.blogspot.co.uk, etc.) is affected by Twitter's ban, and blog posts via those feeds may be tweeted without getting Twitter's dire warning page thrown up in your face first. If you like my blog and wish to help me convince Twitter to take it off their blacklist, please visit https://support.twitter.com/forms/spam, click on the "can't tweet a link" button, and specify http://kimiversonheadlee.blogspot.com as the "problematic link." Thanks! [Preface, 3A, 4A4, 4B1, 4B2]

Media kit. A portfolio consisting of a collection of images and text describing a book, book series, or author that has been assembled for promotional purposes. The media kit may exist in physical or digital form. [4A2, 4A10, 4I]

Metadata. Any attribute you wish to define about your book, either embedded within the e-book's HTML coding itself or using predefined fields on the book's setup pages at companies such as Bowker, IngramSpark, KDP, and Nook Press. [2F1, 3B]

MOBI. Amazon's proprietary e-book format for Kindle devices. [2F1, 4G]

NetGalley (https://netgalley.uservoice.com/knowledgebase/topics/16110-for-publishers-and-authors). A website that facilitates the distribution of digital ARCs for review. [4J4]

Nook Press (https://www.nookpress.com/), a.k.a. Nook. Barnes & Noble's platform for publishing books formatted for display on Nook devices, formerly known as PubIt. [1A, 1D, 1E1, 2A1, 2D, 2E2, 4F3, 4G, 4K1, 4K2, 4L2, 4M2, 4N2, 4O]

NPR sponsorship (http://www.npr.org/about-npr/187533209/major-gifts). A resource for anyone wishing to pursue a major sponsorship with National Public Radio. [4A7]

PayPal (https://www.paypal.com/home). Online payment collection and distribution agency. Some publishers and book e-tailers require authors to establish verified PayPal accounts for the purpose of distributing royalty payments. [1B]

People Reads (http://www.peoplereads.com/list-your-ebook). A free book-marketing service consisting of either email, website, or other social media promotion, or some combination thereof. Paid marketing options for guaranteed advertising placement may also be available. [4F1]

Period Images (http://www.periodimages.com/). A website for obtaining licenses for stock photos. [2E1]

Permafree. In publishing parlance, this is an e-book that is offered free in perpetuity across all e-tailer platforms. [4E, 4F1, 4F2, 4G, 4N2]

PFH, a.k.a. per finished hour. A type of audiobook contract in ACX whereby the rights holder pays the producer an upfront fee upon completion of the production that is computed as the negotiated PFH rate multiplied by the finished length of the audiobook in hours and minutes. [2G1, 2G2]

Print-on-demand, a.k.a. POD. The printing process whereby a book is printed, bound, and shipped upon receipt of a customer's order. A customer may be an individual or a company such as a bookstore. [2A1, 2E3, 4A1, 4H, 4N1]

Producer. In audiobook production, this is the project's narrator. The producer is responsible for all aspects of recording, editing, and finishing the audiobook and may be either the rights holder or a separate person or production team. [2G1, 2G2]

"Promoting a Box Set with BookBub Ads" (https://insights.bookbub.com/promoting-a-box-set-with-bookbub-ads-case-study/). A case study by BookBub Industry Marketing Manager Diana Urban. [4F3]

Pronoun (https://pronoun.com/). Third-party distributor of e-book content to major e-tailer sites such as Nook Press and Kobo. [4O]

Pronoun retailer distribution fees (http://support.pronoun.com/knowledge_base/topics/what-are-the-retailers-distribution-fees). A resource for determining a Pronoun user's net earnings on e-book sales made at a given retailer. [4O]

Publisher's Lunch (http://lunch.publishersmarketplace.com/). A daily digest of top news in the publishing industry distributed to members of PublishersMarketplace (http://www.publishersmarketplace.com/). [1B]

Publishers Weekly (http://www.publishersweekly.com/). An American weekly trade magazine serving the publishing industry that's been in continuous production since 1872. Although it began life as a compendium of industry news, these days its primary focus is book reviews. [2G2, 4A1]

"Publishing Using a Pen Name" (http://www.derekhaines.ch/vandal/2012/04/publishing-using-a-pen-name/). A blog post by author Derek Haines. [3B]

QR code, a.k.a. quick response code. A specialized bar code that can encode a hyperlink to a product page, video, email address, plain text, etc. [4A9, 4M]

QR Stuff (http://www.qrstuff.com/). A website that provides free and fancy-for-a-fee QR codes. [4M3]

QuickBooks (https://quickbooks.intuit.com/). Business accounting software produced by Intuit Inc. [1A, 1B]

Rafflecopter (https://www.rafflecopter.com/pricing). A giveaway management service that has free as well as paid options. [4A11, 4H]

Random.org (https://www.random.org/). A website for selecting a true random number based on user-specified minimum (default=1) and maximum (default=100) number boundaries. [4H]

Razzle Dazzle Stock (http://www.razzdazzstock.com/index). A website for obtaining licenses for stock photos. [2E1]

Read Cheaply (http://readcheaply.com/partners/). A free book-marketing service consisting of either email, website, or other social media promotion, or some combination thereof. Paid marketing options for guaranteed advertising placement may also be available. [4F2]

Reading Deals (http://readingdeals.com/submit-ebook). A free book-marketing service consisting of either email, website, or other social media promotion, or some combination thereof. Paid marketing options for guaranteed advertising placement may also be available. [4F1]

Relinks.me (http://relinks.me/). A website for creating a free universal Amazon link and matching QR code for any product in the Amazon catalog. The site stays afloat by adding its own Amazon affiliate tag to your product's link. [4M2, 4M3].

Rights holder. The entity—the author, author's representative, or publisher—who owns the rights to produce a manuscript in a given format such as digital, print, or audiobook. [2G1, 2G2]

Romance Lives Forever (http://romancelivesforever.blogspot.com/p/guest-blogger-faqs.html). A blog that's a free book-marketing service consisting of website and social media promotion. [4F1]

Romance Reader, The (http://www.theromancereviews.com/advertise.php). A paid book-marketing service consisting of either email, website, or other social media promotion, or some combination thereof. Free promotion opportunities may be available too. [4F2]

Romance Readers Club (http://romancereadersclub.com/for-authors/). A free book-marketing service consisting of either email, website, or other social media promotion, or some combination thereof. Paid marketing options for guaranteed advertising placement may also be available. [4F1]

Romance Rock Stars (http://romancerockstars.com/index.php/author-services/). A free book-marketing service consisting of either email, website, or other social media promotion, or some combination thereof. Paid marketing options for guaranteed advertising placement may also be available. [4F1]

Roundteam (https://roundteam.co/). A Twitter content management service. [4A11]

Royalty-free license. A type of license for music, photos, illustrations, videos, and other media that permits the user—for a onetime fee—to adapt and replicate an image, song, or video in whatever manner the user wishes, including commercial applications, though sometimes restrictions are imposed upon the number of downloads the media receives. [2E1, 2G2]

Royalty share. A type of contract in ACX whereby the rights holder and producer split an audiobook's net royalties 50-50 for each sale. [2G1]

RWA (https://www.rwa.org/), a.k.a. Romance Writers of America. An American nonprofit organization dedicated to serving the needs of authors who write romance genre fiction. An author must possess an active RWA membership to be eligible for membership in any of RWA's more than 145 local and online chapters. [1B, 1C, 3C3]

RWA National (https://www.rwa.org/p/cm/ld/fid=569). The annual conference organized by the Romance Writers of America. Its location rotates among major US cities, though it is held in New York City—for Manhattan's proximity to the headquarters of major US publishing houses—on average once every five years. [1B, 3C3]

S corporation. A type of corporate structure for small businesses. For a precise definition, please consult your lawyer or an online service such as LegalZoom. [1A]

Scribd (https://www.scribd.com/). A subscription e-book and audiobook distribution platform. Subscribers also have access to sheet music and other documents that have been uploaded by other subscribers. [4G]

"Selecting Browse Categories" (https://kdp.amazon.com/help?topicId=A200PDGPEIQX41). A general reference that includes links to keyword tables by Amazon category (i. e. BISAC subject codes). Links to some of the most common keyword tables are found in this section: [4K2]

SEO, a.k.a. search engine optimization. The process of affecting the visibility of a website or a web page in a web search engine's unpaid results. In theory, the more higher ranked and more frequently a site appears in the search results list, the more visitors—and potential customers—it will receive from the search engine's users. [4C]

"SEO Image Optimization: 10 Proven Ways To Boost Yours" (http://madlemmings.com/2016/01/11/seo-image-optimization/). A blog post about search engine optimization for images by Taylor Manning. [4C]

"Should Authors Blog?" (http://mfrw.blogspot.com/2015/10/why-blog.html). A blog post by MFRW founder Kayelle Allen. [4B]

Smashwords (https://www.smashwords.com/). Third-party distributor of e-book content to major e-tailer sites such as Nook Press and Kobo. [1E1, 2A1, 2F, 2F1, 4F3, 4G, 4N2, 4O]

Smashwords affiliate program (https://www.smashwords.com/about/supportfaq#Affiliate). A resource for Smashwords users contemplating affiliate participation. [4O]

Smashwords distribution information (https://www.smashwords.com/distribution). A resource for Smashwords users that explains the site's premium catalog and other aspects of the e-book distribution process. [4O]

Sole proprietorship. A type of corporate structure for small businesses. For a precise definition, please consult your lawyer or an online service such as LegalZoom. [1A]

Spread. In book layout terminology, this refers to a pair of pages representing an open book. [2F2]

StreetLib (https://www.streetlib.com/meetstreetlibus/). A third-party e-book distributor. [4O]

System Support Services Inc. The S-corporation of author Kim Iverson Headlee, also trading as S3I. [1A]

Taber, Deb (http://www.debtaber.com/editing-services). The primary developmental editor and proofreader employed by Kim Iverson Headlee. [2B]

Tagline. In writing parlance, this is the hook or "elevator pitch" for your book. The shorter and snappier the tagline, the better. [2D, 4I, 4J4]

Thalia.de (http://www.thalia.de/shop/home/show/). The online retail website of German brick-and-mortar bookstore chain Thalia. [4A4]

"The Do's and Don'ts of Reviewing on Amazon!" (http://awordwithtraci.com/the-dos-and-donts-of-reviewing-on-amazon/). A blog post by author Traci Sanders. [4J3]

The eReader Cafe (http://theereadercafe.com/promote-your-books/). A free book-marketing service consisting of either email, website, or other social media promotion, or some combination thereof. Paid marketing options for guaranteed advertising placement may also be available. [4F1]

"The Indie Authors' Guide to DIY Audiobooks" (http://booklife.com/publish/audio/06/29/2015/the-indie-authors-guide-to-diy-audiobooks.html). A blog post by *BookLife* contributor Ryan Joe. [2G2]

"Think You Couldn't Possibly Lose Your Amazon Publishing Account? Think Again." (https://the-active-voice.com/2016/06/16/think-you-couldnt-possibly-lose-your-amazon-publishing-account-think-again/). An article by Becca Mills. [4O]

Triberr (http://triberr.com/). A post-sharing service for bloggers that offers free and paid service options. [4A11, 4B1, 4B2, 4L2]

Trim size. The length and width, expressed in inches or millimeters, to which interior pages are trimmed. If you plan to create your book's interior layout using Adobe InDesign, its default for specifying trim size is the pica, a typographic unit of measure corresponding to one-sixth of an inch (i.e., 4.233 millimeters or 0.166 inches). [4H, 4N1]

TurboTax Business (https://turbotax.intuit.com/small-business-taxes/). Tax preparation software that comes in a variety of subspecies for estates and small businesses. [1A, 1B, 1D]

Tweet Jukebox (http://www.tweetjukebox.com/). A Twitter content management service. [4A11]

"Twitter's New 140 Character Updates and How to Take Advantage of It" (http://blog.socedo.com/twitters-new-140-character-updates-and-how-to-take-advantage-of-it/). A blog post by Teena Thach. [4L3]

Videos by O (http://videosbyo.blogspot.com/). A producer of book trailers, animated book covers, and other graphic design services. [4A8]

Visuallead (http://visuallead.com). A service for embedding an image in your QR codes. [4M3]

Washington Romance Writers (http://wrwdc.com/), a.k.a. WRW. A chapter of the Romance Writers of America serving the needs of romance authors in the Washington DC region and worldwide. A prospective chapter member must be a member in good standing of RWA. [4H]

"What Else Are Your BookBub Readers Reading?" (https://insights.bookbub.com/what-else-are-your-bookbub-readers-reading/). An infographic describing the category crossover combinations of typical BookBub subscribers. [4F3]

WHOIS (https://www.whois.net/). This tool is used for querying databases that store information about the registered users or assignees of an Internet resource such as a domain name or an IP address block. The protocol stores and delivers database content in a human-readable format. [2A2]

"Why I Refuse to Join Kindle Unlimited" (http://blather.michaelwlucas.com/archives/2703). A blog post by author Michael Lucas. [4O]

"Why Reader Reviews Matter" (https://nowasted-ink.com/2015/07/17/guest-post-why-reader-reviews-matter-by-gail-z-martin/). A blog post by author Gail Z. Martin. [4J1]

Wraparound cover, a.k.a. wrap. A paperback book's cover, which contains a front cover, spine, and back cover; so named because the front image commonly wraps around to the back. [2E3, 4I]

Writer's Digest (http://www.writersdigest.com/). An American magazine founded in 1920 under the name *Successful Writing*. It has been known as *Writer's Digest* since March 1921. The intended audience for its market news, tutorials, sponsored contests, and interviews is writers at all career stages. [1B]

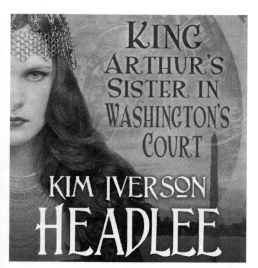

About the Author

KIM HEADLEE LIVES on a farm in southwestern Virginia with her family, cats, goats, Great Pyrenees goat guards, and assorted wildlife. People and creatures come and go, but the cave and the 250-year-old house ruins—the latter having been occupied as recently as the midtwentieth century—seem to be sticking around for a while yet.

http://www.kimheadlee.com
https://twitter.com/KimHeadlee
http://www.facebook.com/kimiversonheadlee

Other published works by Kim Iverson Headlee:

"Kings," a sword & sorcery crossover novella by Kim Iverson Headlee and Patricia Duffy Novak, e-book and paperback, Pendragon Cove Press, 2016.

King Arthur's Sister in Washington's Court by Mark Twain as channeled by Kim Iverson Headlee, illustrated by Jennifer Doneske and Tom Doneske, hardcover, paperback, audiobook, and e-book, Lucky Bat Books, 2015.

Raging Sea: Reckonings, part 1 of The Dragon's Dove Chronicles, book 3, e-book, Pendragon Cove Press, 2015.

Liberty, second edition, with character-totem art by Jessica Headlee, e-book and paperback, Pendragon Cove Press, 2014.

Snow in July, with character-totem art by Jessica Headlee, e-book and paperback, Pendragon Cove Press, 2014.

"The Color of Vengeance," a short story excerpted from *Morning's Journey*, e-book and audiobook, Lucky Bat Books, 2013; paperback, Pendragon Cove Press, 2015.

Morning's Journey, The Dragon's Dove Chronicles, book 2, e-book and paperback, Lucky Bat Books, 2013; cover and interior updated 2014.

Dawnflight, second edition, The Dragon's Dove Chronicles, book 1, e-book, audiobook, and paperback, Lucky Bat Books, 2013; cover and interior updated 2014.

Liberty by Kimberly Iverson, first edition, paperback, HQN Books, Harlequin, 2006.

Dawnflight by Kim Headlee, first edition, paperback, Sonnet Books, Simon & Schuster, 1999.

Forthcoming:

Raging Sea: Enemies and Allies, part 2 of The Dragon's Dove Chronicles, book 3, Pendragon Cove Press.

"The Challenge" graphic novel, episode 2: Final Preparations, Pendragon Cove Press.

Prophecy, the sequel to *Liberty*, Pendragon Cove Press.

Now on Sale!
The Challenge Full-Color Graphic Novel
Episode 1: Dilemmas & Deliberation
Art and Storyboard by Wendy Carey

The Challenge
Graphic Novel
Episode 1
Kindle worldwide
link

Made in the USA
Middletown, DE
10 February 2017